DR. DAVID STOOP

Experiencing GOD Together

Spiritual

Intimacy

In

Marriage

Tyndale House Publishers, Inc.
Wheaton, Illinois

Published in association with the literary agency of Alive Communications, Inc., 1465 Kelly Johnson Blvd., Suite 320, Colorado Springs, CO 80920.

Editor: Vinita Hampton Wright

Library of Congress Cataloging-in-Publication Data

Stoop, David A.
  Experiencing God together : spiritual intimacy in marriage / David Stoop.
    p. cm.
  ISBN 0-8423-5972-9 (alk. paper)
    1. Married people—Religious life. 2. Marriage—religious aspects—Christianity.
3. Intimacy (Psychology)—Religious aspects—Christianity. I. Title.
BV4596.M3S76   1996
248.8'44—dc20   96-5019

Printed in the United States of America

01 00 99 98 97 96
7   6   5   4   3   2   1

CONTENTS

"You know, as a Christian couple, I guess we just felt that we were invulnerable. Nothing could get to us. But over the years, we drifted apart, and then we found out just how vulnerable we were. But it was too late."

I was listening to a young man whose divorce—a divorce he did not want—had just been finalized by the court. We were trying to piece together what had gone wrong over the years, and his comment about invulnerability really struck me. That invincible feeling, which is very strong when we are young, often pervades our attitude toward job, health, and even marriage. Unfortunately, some of us are awakened to the reality that we are vulnerable only after some disaster strikes—financial ruin, a failed marriage, or the onset of serious illness. Divorce had forced this young man to face the fact that a marriage is not automatically protected from trouble just because both partners are Christians.

Divorce had forced him to face the fact that a marriage is not automatically protected just because both partners are Christians.

More couples are realizing earlier in the process that good marriages don't just happen. This truth is often more easily recognized by people involved in a second marriage. The failure of their first marriage has made them more determined to succeed the second time, and they are willing to do the work that is required. One man said to me recently, "If I'd worked even half this hard in my first marriage, we would not only have stayed together, we'd have had a great marriage."

Back in the days when marriages were arranged, some were loving while others were miserable. One of the determining factors was the willingness of both people to do the work necessary to develop a satisfying relationship. With all of our emphasis on romance and spontaneity today, the success of a marriage still depends on each partner's willingness to do whatever work is required. This work involves every area of our married life—money, children, sexuality, careers, and spirituality.

I've always felt invulnerable when it came to my health. I used to be proud of the fact that I was addicted to nonexercise! If someone asked me why, I would say that the extra few days one might live were not worth the pain today. After all, "I'm healthy, and I plan to stay that way." That was my attitude until about two years ago. One day while I was playing golf, I noticed that I couldn't squat down to line up a putt. When I finally did get down there, I could hardly get back up again. So I decided to start some physical exercise—not so I could live longer but so I could live better. I had just come face-to-face with that unpleasant reality we call the aging process.

I signed up at a men's gym nearby, and on my first day I was assigned a trainer. For over an hour, Jeff paced me through different disciplined exercises and explained how each one would help me feel better. I rode the exercise bike for thirty minutes, mainly because he made me slow down so that I could last that long. Within a few days he had introduced me to the rest of the routine that would do me the most good, given my condition and my goals.

I've stuck with it! Sometimes two, three, or four times a week, but I'm there every week, doing what I had once decided never to do. And after about six months, I found I could squat down again and line up my putts.

What I discovered about my physical vulnerability exists in every area of my life. And it is especially true in my marriage. The good that I want to experience is not going to happen unless I do the work. That requires some time evaluating, looking straight at my weaknesses as a husband and at the areas of the marriage that need strengthening. And in an area like spirituality and how it relates to the husband-wife team, we must take the time to examine, set up our "program," and get to work.

The trouble is, most of us are unaware of how out of shape we are in this area. We don't see many marriages in which spiritual intimacy is modeled. We hardly know where to begin, or what to expect.

The apostle Paul writes, "Spend your time and energy in the exercise of keeping spiritually fit. Bodily exercise is all right, but spiritual exercise is much more important and is a tonic for all you do. So exercise yourself spiritually, and practice being a better Christian because that will help you not only now in this life, but in the next life too" (1 Tim. 4:7-8).

Perhaps because I was involved with physical exercise I had a fresh understanding of what Paul was saying about spiritual exercise. Is there a spiritual "routine" that one can follow? I believe there is. For centuries, we have called these activities "spiritual disciplines." Some of them are familiar to us; others have been neglected, due to the changes of modern culture and some gaps in our understanding of theology and church history. All of the disciplines outlined in this book are in line with orthodox, Christian faith and have been practiced by believers since the days of Jesus and the early church.

Usually, when we read about spirituality or are involved in a Bible study about it, we apply what we learn to ourselves as individuals. But do these truths about spiritual growth apply to two individuals who have "become one"? We believe that they do—and in powerful ways. When two people who are bonded by the marriage covenant are actively seeking God *as a couple,* a whole new realm of spiritual life opens up to them.

Jan and I do not hold ourselves out as successful examples of each of these disciplines. We have tried each of them; we were successful with some and failed miserably with others. So we are in the process with you. When we have failed with one of the disciplines, we have backed up and slowed down the process. Our personal goal is not to arrive at some destination, which seems impossible to us at times. Our goal is to be in the process—to be on the road toward that destination we call spiritual intimacy. And each little step we take in the right direction becomes very satisfying.

EVALUATE THE SPIRITUAL INTIMACY OF YOUR MARRIAGE

The best beginning is an evaluation. My trainer helped me assess my physical condition so that he could tell me where to begin my routine so that I wouldn't get discouraged and quit. We need to do the same thing with our marriage. So we've devised a special *Marriage Intimacy Inventory* for you and your spouse. You don't get a score or a pass/fail grade—it simply gives you a picture of where you are today. We suggest that you retake it every six months or so and check your results with the previous tests to chart your progress. If there are no changes, it may mean you've been too busy with other things and need to get refocused on this aspect of your marriage. If there have been positive changes, that's a good sign of growth and greater health for your relationship. It takes a while, but eventually the benefits will come.

MARRIAGE INTIMACY INVENTORY

There are two parts to this inventory. The first part helps us evaluate ten areas of intimacy that can exist in a marriage. The second part focuses on more specific aspects of spiritual intimacy. You may make photocopies of the inventory or you may use different colored pens to mark your responses. Each of you should finish part I before going on to part 2.

PART I: TEN TYPES OF INTIMACY

Place a check mark in the blank that applies to your relationship, as you understand it.

Types of Intimacy	I think it needs improvement	I think my mate thinks it needs improvement	I think we are both satisfied
1. Sexual Intimacy	_____	_____	_____
2. Emotional Intimacy (Being tuned in to each other)	_____	_____	_____
3. Intellectual Intimacy (Sharing ideas)	_____	_____	_____
4. Social Intimacy (Enjoying socializing)	_____	_____	_____
5. Recreational Intimacy (Sharing experiences of fun and play)	_____	_____	_____
6. Creative Intimacy (Sharing in the creating of things)	_____	_____	_____
7. Crisis Intimacy (Closeness in coping with problems and pain)	_____	_____	_____
8. Work Intimacy (Closeness in sharing common tasks)	_____	_____	_____
9. Conflict Intimacy (Facing and struggling with differences)	_____	_____	_____
10. Spiritual Intimacy	_____	_____	_____

After you go through the list, evaluate where you spend the most energy in your marriage. Number these ten types of intimacy from 1 to 10, with 1 representing the area in which you expend the most energy and 10 representing the area in which you expend the least energy. Do this individually, then compare answers and discuss where you differ and where you agree.

PART 2: SPIRITUAL INTIMACY INVENTORY
The following is a self-study, which may be used in several ways.

1. It can be used individually or as a couple and referred to every six months or so to check on your progress.
2. It can be shared with your partner and discussed on a regular basis.
3. It can be shared in a small group and referred to every few months.

Each question can be answered by a simple yes or no. Make a photocopy, so that each of you can answer separately. In the space provided, write out your answer to each question.

1. Do you have a regular time given to personal devotions each day? _____
2. Is God real to you when you pray? _____
3. Do you make it a point to speak to God every day—before you speak to anyone else? _____
4. Are your last thoughts before going to sleep directed toward God? _____
5. Have you learned to pray frequently throughout the day? _____
6. Have you learned to be still and listen to God's voice? _____
7. Does God speak to you through the Bible as you read it? _____
8. Are you entirely honest with God as you face your sins in his presence? _____
9. Are you willing to let God show you the faults and weaknesses of your heart? _____

10. Do you turn quickly to God when you are conscious of having sinned? _____
11. Can you pray with your spouse? _____
12. Are you interested in praying with your spouse? _____
13. Does gratitude to God find frequent expression in your prayers? _____
14. Can you pray with your spouse whenever one of you needs to? _____
15. Do you ever fast? _____
16. Have you ever fasted at the same time as your spouse fasted? _____
17. Do you understand the meaning of fasting? _____
18. Do you talk with your spouse about your tithes and offerings? _____
19. Are you able to pray for your enemies? _____
20. Do you ever pray together for the conversion of someone who doesn't know Christ? _____
21. Do the two of you ever read the Bible to each other? _____
22. Have the two of you ever read and discussed a book on prayer? _____
23. Have the two of you ever read and discussed a book on fasting? _____
24. Have you learned to meditate prayerfully on God's Word? _____
25. Have you received a convincing answer to prayer during the last year? _____
26. Has God ever dramatically answered a prayer that you and your spouse have agreed upon? _____
27. Can you discuss openly with your spouse what you believe God wants you to do? _____
28. Do you pray for your spouse regularly throughout the day? _____
29. Does your spouse share your perspective on worship? _____
30. Do you enjoy worshiping together? _____
31. Do you ever have a private time of worship together? _____

32. Do you pray together for your pastor and your church? _____
33. Do you have friends who pray for you daily? _____
34. Are you working on being faithful in the little things? _____
35. Are you able to pray for and with others with whom you disagree? _____
36. Can you pray with your spouse when you disagree? _____
Number of **yes** answers: _____
Number of **no** answers: _____

When each of you has finished, compare the results and discuss the areas in which your responses are different from each other or areas one or both of you felt were weak.

This inventory gives you an idea of where your marriage is in terms of intimacy, spiritual and otherwise. You and your spouse can now discuss what you would like to see improved. Each couple will have their own areas of need and priority. Depending on your life circumstances, your personalities, and the specific needs each of you is experiencing, some areas of intimacy will be more important than others. The goal is not that you accomplish items 1 through 36 all at once! Decide together which aspects of your life together you would like to see strengthened and developed. Then explore each of these areas in the chapters to come.

ONE

Holey, Wholly, Holy:
Can Marriage Be Spiritual?

SUE has taught the women's Bible study every Tuesday morning in her church for the past five years. Each year it has grown so that now attendance averages just a little under two hundred, almost as much as Sunday morning church attendance. And each week this past year some woman in the study has become a Christian.

Sue's husband, Tom, has been an elder in the church, and last year he was chairman of the elders. He is not ashamed of his relationship with Christ. He is respected not only by everyone in the church but also by his coworkers. To everyone who knows them, Tom and Sue appear to have it all together; undoubtedly, they are the envy of those who wish that they, also, could serve God as a couple.

But now they sit across from me in my office, and Sue announces that she has fallen in love with someone else. She and Tom are here to discuss getting a divorce. Tom certainly isn't comfortable with the conversation, but he insists upon trying to understand Sue's feelings. They both want help in knowing how

1

to handle the situation so that their children will go through the least suffering possible and people in the church will be more accepting of the inevitable.

Of course, I'm curious about what went wrong. Sue says, "We just grew apart, I guess. The spark has been gone for several years." I ask them if they have ever prayed together in their marriage of fifteen years. Sue's response: "I tried, but Tom never wanted to. He seemed too uncomfortable, so I just gave up and poured myself into my women's Bible study." Then she adds quietly, "I guess I'll have to take a leave from teaching, at least until this is all over."

All of us know people who, as individuals, appear to be in close relationship with God; yet they are miserable in their marriage and find it impossible to share spiritually with their spouse. Although we understand this and may even accept it, some of us long for more. If spiritual growth can't have an impact upon our marriage, how real is it?

All of us know couples who seem to be close to God individually, yet who find it impossible to share spiritually with each other.

Perhaps you have struggled with this issue. How is it that you can experience more of God, yet that spirituality doesn't seem to touch your marriage? Is it possible for us to deepen both our marital intimacy and our intimacy with God? Is this even a realistic goal?

With very few exceptions, all the books that focus on our spiritual growth are concerned only with the relationship between the individual and God. They answer questions like, "How can I grow closer to God?" and "How can I experience more of the reality of God in my life?" These are valid concerns, and we shouldn't treat them lightly. But what about the spiritual health of our marriage? Is God concerned only with our spiritual growth as individuals, perhaps hoping that this deepening spirituality will somehow spill over and affect the marriage? Our overall silence about spiritual growth within marriage appears to give credence to the attitude that spirituality is a concern only for individuals.

Jan and I believe not only that spiritual growth is related to our marriage but that marriage can be the context in which the depth and reality of our spirituality is tested and developed most effectively. Our intent is to provide help for people who are interested in developing spiritual intimacy within their marriage and for those who want to know more about how God can work with a couple that wants to seek him *together*.

HOLEY MATRIMONY:
WHAT'S WRONG WITH THIS PICTURE?

There are a lot of "holes" in the institution of marriage these days. Even though a myriad of books is published each year about how to improve marriage, in the bigger picture our culture is moving away from being marriage centered. It appears that the concern of our age is not really how to have better marriages but how to have better divorces. Magazine articles, movies, TV sitcoms, and even professional journals and research seem aimed, not at improving marriages, but at helping people normalize the experience of divorce.

Unfortunately, what happens in our culture also infects our churches. According to the statistics, even though the divorce-centered attitude may not be discussed as openly within the church, the percentage of people getting divorced there is almost identical to the percentage of people getting divorced in the general population.

An example of our culture's growing concern with "quality" divorce is well articulated by one secular author, Melinda Blau, who wrote the recent book, *Families Apart.* Blau is the award-winning writer of the "New Family" column in *Child* magazine. The major emphasis of both her column and her book is how to help people divorce better. She insists that we stop "romanticizing marriage and the nuclear family"[1] and begin to work on the realities of emerging forms of "new families." What she is saying and writing represents the growing number and volume of voices speaking for divorce-centeredness in our culture. These voices say that we need to accept divorce as a way of life and learn how to make it painless.

In *Fatherless America,* author David Blankenhorn notes that at a recent national convention of the American Association of Marriage and Family Therapists, there was not a single workshop that even used the word *marriage.* In the list of workshops and presentations, there were 43 major topics to be covered during that convention, and within those 43 topics, 234 subtopics were listed. Not once was the word *marriage* used in the title of any workshop or presentation. Blankenhorn suggests that if that organization were naming itself today, it probably wouldn't even use the word *marriage.* It's a sad commentary on our culture when those who call themselves professional marriage therapists simply avoid the word *marriage.*

Rather than maintaining and improving marriage, we are far more interested in defining "new families" that are emerging in our divorce-oriented culture. Researchers try to make it seem that the single-parent family works, even though all the evidence tells us that both the single parents and the children suffer. They also look at alternative family styles (including same-sex parents), gender issues, and other nonnuclear and nontraditional family issues. Perhaps our desire to create a vision of a good di-

1. Quoted by David Blankenhorn, in *Fatherless America* (New York: Basic Book, 1995), 159.

vorce is an extension of the pursuit of personal freedom that seems so intrinsic to being American today.

We are also becoming more centered on the individual. We watch people in sitcoms, movies, and real life who are wrestling with the question, What's in it for me? There is little being said today about commitment and sacrifice. And even that is often drowned out by the subtle and not-so-subtle messages of our "me-first" society.

But some of us are different! We are making distinctive choices about what is important in life. We want to know how to experience more of God. We are very much aware of the growing pressures to "look out for yourself," but we have chosen to fight against these pressures and seek what God would have for us, as individuals and as partners in marriage.

The True Foundations of Family

In the second chapter of Genesis, "the Lord God said, 'It isn't good for man to be alone; I will make a companion for him, a helper suited to his needs'" (v.18).

Now think a moment about what God is saying here. Adam wasn't really alone. He had all of creation around him—and he had a perfect relationship with God! But God said, "Adam is alone." Obviously, his being alone had nothing to do with his relationship with God, or even with the rest of creation. There was something important missing. There was no other being like Adam.

We also need to understand this passage in the context of the Hebrew viewpoint. Our Western way of thinking is greatly influenced by Greek thought, whereby we divide body from spirit and spirit from soul. In the Hebrew way of thinking, these divisions did not exist—everything was a part of the whole. When God said it wasn't good for Adam to be alone, he meant that *in every way possible* it wasn't good. It wasn't good physically, for there was no partner for Adam. It wasn't good emotionally, for there was no creature like Adam with whom he could share himself. And it wasn't good spiritually, even though Adam had a perfect relationship with God. Something critical was missing—there was an empty space next to Adam. In the Hebrew context, when God said it wasn't good for Adam to be alone, he was referring to Adam's total personhood. In creating Eve as a "suitable helper" to Adam, God was creating a companion for Adam—in every sense. Eve was not merely Adam's sexual complement; neither was she just a companion who could help him with the many tasks of life. Eve was the only creature who shared Adam's spiritual capabilities; together they could commune with God.

In creating Eve, God also created marriage, for in Genesis 2:25, Eve is referred to as "his wife." Thus, on the sixth day of creation, Adam, Eve, and marriage came to be. And only after all had been created did God announce that "it was excellent in every way. This ended the sixth day" (Gen. 1:31). Marriage is a part of God's creation that was pronounced "good." Notice that there were no children until Genesis 4. In the very beginning, the husband-wife relationship, not children, defined the marriage.

In helping families work through their problems, I've found that the marriage itself is the primary relationship to consider as we understand how families work. Our culture has begun to view families as more child-centered; it is common for a couple to gradually shift the focus of their energy and decision making to the children. It's easy to make this shift because we desire to be good parents. But when the children are the primary focus, the marriage will always suffer, and then the children will suffer. The best thing we can do to help our children become healthy adults is to keep marriage our priority. This is the way families work best, because it's the way God designed the family. A strong marriage gives our children a secure place and helps them find the freedom to develop their own lives.

Family around the World

It's interesting how other cultures define the primary relationship within a family. In most Asian cultures, the primary relationship is between the mother and oldest son. This has some very interesting ramifications when that son eventually marries. In such a setup, a woman's relationship to her mother-in-law is nothing to joke about—it's serious business. In some African cultures, the primary relationship is brother to brother. In some Arab cultures, the primary relationship is between the father and eldest son. None of these primary relationship patterns follow the biblical design.

In the past, Western culture has focused on the husband-wife relationship because of the biblical foundation that existed in American and western European cultures. But as we lose touch with our biblical roots, our whole sense of what makes family *family* is open to attack and reinterpretation. We see this going on around us every day. But the truth is, families work best when they are marriage based.

WHOLLY MATRIMONY: WHY SPIRITUAL INTIMACY IN MARRIAGE?

When God made Eve, he could have made her from the dust of the earth, just as he had made Adam. But God made her from Adam's body. That's why Adam exclaimed in Genesis 2:23, "She is part of my own bone and flesh!" The Hebrew writer goes on to tell us that "this explains why a man leaves his father and mother and is joined to his wife in such a way that the two become one person" (Gen. 2:24). There is a total union—a "wholly" union, if you will—between a husband and wife that encompasses all—body, mind, emotion, soul, and spirit. If you leave anything out, you have less than what God intended.

What Does It Mean to Be Spiritual?

Before we consider the question, "Why spiritual intimacy in marriage?" we need to define what we mean—and what we don't mean—by "spiritual intimacy." Often, we think of the spiritually minded person as one who has repressed all desire, especially physical desires for pleasure. I remember thinking, as a young pastor, that only the old people seemed to be really "spiritual"—only they had the time to focus deeply on the inner aspects of the spiritual life. I was the pastor, so I was expected to have some level of spirituality, but even then not the same as the older people in the church—they were the spiritual giants, supposedly.

The other common perception of spirituality I struggled with during those earlier years was that a truly spiritual person had great faith, even though he or she seemed to neglect other aspects of life. It appeared that marriage and family took second place to spiritual giftedness and calling. Even physical appearance was neglected in favor of prayer and devotional life. To the younger members of the church, such an expression of spiritual intimacy with God held no attractiveness, at least not for the present. They wanted to have fun and enjoy life when they were young, and somehow spirituality didn't seem fun or enjoyable.

Sometimes we define spirituality or spiritual intimacy in terms of personal discipline. We look at those people whose personalities are more structured, who are able to have their private devotions early *every* morning. They read their One Year Bible on schedule. And they are more than willing to encourage those who aren't so disciplined to "become more mature." But often these people, instead of developing a deepened sense of the presence, power, and grace of God, only find a rigid, legalistic form of spirituality, which is also quite unattractive.

It's much easier, based on our experiences and observations, to define what it is we *don't* like about spirituality and spiritual intimacy than to define something that is attractive and meaningful about them.

A simple definition of intimacy that Jan and I have used is "the joyful union that comes when two people learn together how to give love and how to accept love."[2] If we were to modify that definition so that it encompassed spiritual intimacy, we could say, "spiritual intimacy is the joyful union that comes when two people learn *together* how to relate to God and to experience God at work in their lives in very practical, specific ways." This kind of intimacy is the ability to come *together* and, in that shared context, relate intimately with God and with each other.

A term that is often used as a synonym for spiritual intimacy is "spirituality." Dallas Willard defines spirituality in human beings as

> not an extra or "superior" mode of existence. It's not a hidden stream of separate reality, a separate life running parallel to our bodily existence. It does not consist of special "inward" acts even though it has an inner aspect. It is, rather, a relationship of our embodied selves to God that has the natural and irrepressible effect of making us alive to the Kingdom of God—here and now in the material world.[3]

He goes on to say that spirituality, or spiritual intimacy, is not opposed to the rest of us—our body, mind, and emotions. He makes a strong point that "spirituality is simply the holistic quality of human life as it was meant to be, at the center of which is our relation to God."[4] We could take his point and justifiably say that spiritual intimacy is a quality of marriage as it was meant to

2. David Stoop and Jan Stoop, *The Intimacy Factor* (Nashville: Thomas Nelson, 1992), 13.
3. Dallas Willard, *The Spirit of the Disciplines* (San Francisco: Harper, 1988), 31.
4. Ibid., 77.

be in the beginning, with God as an intimate part of everything we do and experience.

Spiritual intimacy is a quality of marriage as it was meant to be, with God as an intimate part of everything we do and experience.

Missing What We Used to Have

From the Genesis account, we know that neither Adam nor Eve "was embarrassed or ashamed." They did not experience fear or shame or defensiveness, but a comfortable openness with one another. In addition, together they shared everything with God. Apparently they met God in the Garden each evening and shared the events of their day with him. Undoubtedly, this spiritual intimacy involved every aspect of their lives—their work, their play, the relationship they had with one another. It would seem natural that they would talk with God about all the fascinating things they were exploring and discovering in their physical relationship with each other. This kind of openness with each other and with God was the way things were meant to be.

But the human rebellion and disobedience in Genesis 3 is a reality. Verse 7 says, "And as they ate it, suddenly they became aware of their nakedness, and were embarrassed." Later, when God came to meet with them in the Garden, they were afraid and hid themselves. So we see that when sin entered into the human experience, it also brought fear, shame, self-consciousness, and defensiveness.

These negative, confusing aspects of human relationships are why many writers and teachers, in addressing spirituality and spiritual disciplines, suggest that marriage is too complicated a situation for conscious work on spiritual intimacy to take place.[5] Perhaps this is part of the reason all of the books on spirituality are directed at the individual. Fear, shame, self-consciousness, and defensiveness easily get in the way of any kind of intimacy in marriage, and especially in the deep matters of the spirit. But this difficulty shouldn't prevent us from approaching this important area of our life together.

What Makes Your Marriage Christian?

As a therapist who enjoys working with married couples, I have had many of my presuppositions challenged and destroyed by what I have experienced in my counseling office. In far too many cases, couples have referred to their marriage as being Christian, but the only thing that made their marriage Christian was the type of wedding ceremony they had chosen, or the fact that they went to the same church. Most have never even thought about what it is that makes a marriage Christian.

How does the reality of Christ within your personal life affect your marriage? Most people answer that question by saying, "Well, we have a Christian marriage because we're both Christians." Or, "We go to church together." But when they go on to describe what happens between them, there is nothing evident that makes their marriage uniquely Christian.

To me, what makes a marriage Christian is that *we as a couple are seeking to restore what was lost back in Genesis.* We become whole people again through the work of Christ, and our marriage becomes fully what it was designed to be—a complete, satisfying union of two people before God. In a marriage that is growing spiritually, both partners make the choice regularly to confront not only the shame, defensiveness, and fear that any two people are going to encounter in an intimate relationship, but also the brokenness in their relationship with God. We are en-

5. See Paul Stevens, *Marriage Spirituality* (Downers Grove, Ill.: InterVarsity Press, 1989), 42. He notes a number of these writers and their reservations about bringing spiritual disciplines into the marriage relationship.

deavoring to restore some part of what Adam and Eve shared together with God in the very beginning.

What makes a marriage Christian is that we as a couple are seeking to restore what was lost back in Genesis.

In a marriage that is Christian, we are to seek to restore that spiritual intimacy with God, together as well as individually. Although we can't go back to the Garden, we can recapture *within our new life in Christ* some of the marital joy that was originally experienced through intimacy with God.

Unless that search for spiritual intimacy with God is part of our behavior as a couple, there is little else that distinguishes a marriage as being truly Christian. In the chapters to come, we will explore twelve different ways in which spiritual intimacy can be developed—between marriage partners and their Creator. We'll look at some practical ways to make some of these activities a part of marriage.

HOLY MATRIMONY:
PUTTING FAITH INTO PRACTICE TOGETHER

Several years ago Jan and I were listening to a series of messages given by Ron Cline, then head of a missionary radio station of HCJB in Quito, Ecuador. His series was organized around the idea of joining the parade. The parade he described was one that spanned the centuries. He started to name those in the parade. He began with Peter and continued with the apostle Paul. He walked us through time as he touched on other great people of faith in church history. Then he described several incredible people in the parade, people he had met in his missionary travels around the world. One lived in Eastern Europe, another in Russia, while others were from other remote parts of the world.

He painted a picture, suggesting that all of these people were marching by in a great parade, celebrating and participating in God's activities in the world. He said that we can stand there on the sidewalk and watch the parade go by. We might get excited about the parade and tell others about it, yet remain on the curb, watching. Or we can go home and forget about the parade, chalking it up as just one more experience in life. *Or we can step off the curb and join the parade.* We can join God in his work in the world today. We can become participants! Both Jan and I were greatly moved by his messages. Later on as we were talking about what Ron had said, one of us said to the other, "Do you think we've stepped off the curb?"

We wondered how God wanted to be involved with us as a couple. How could we step off the curb—together? We set off in search of a description of this process so that couples like us could determine whether or not they have stepped off the curb and joined God in the parade of his mighty actions. Here are five truths (not to be confused with how-tos) we identified that describe what goes into "joining the parade":

1. We must recognize that God is already at work all around us.
2. Because of the high priority God places on marriage, he cares deeply about us and our marriage, and he invites us as a married couple to join him in his work—already in progress.
3. There are a variety of ways—called spiritual disciplines— we can participate with God, and each of them can deepen our sense of intimacy with each other and, as a couple, with God.
4. These spiritual disciplines will require at least two things

from us: First, that we face our own fears and defenses, especially those we encounter in our marriage relationship; and second, that we adjust our priorities and activities.

5. The deepening experience of our spiritual intimacy with God together will prepare us for a life of obedience, especially when we encounter the "dark nights of the soul."

How do these five truths work out in the reality of day-to-day living, especially in the context of marriage?

Truth #1: God Is Already at Work All around Us

I still remember a particular sermon I preached early in my years as an associate pastor. It was based on the story of Gideon and how God took his small army and kept whittling it down until Gideon was left with only three hundred men. And with those three hundred men God won a great victory. The point I made was that God doesn't *need* us to accomplish his purposes in history, but he *wants* us to participate with him. After I had finished, I remember suddenly thinking about the many sermons I had heard as a young boy that told how God really needed us in order to do what he wanted to do in the world. I wondered whether or not what I had just preached was biblically accurate. When the senior pastor complimented me on my sermon, saying that he agreed with me, I breathed an inward sigh of relief. God's working in the world *doesn't* depend on me; yet the God of the universe invites my participation. Jesus tells us very clearly about how God is at work in this world. He said, after he healed the man by the pool of Bethesda, "My Father is always at his work to this very day, and I, too, am working" (John 5:17, NIV).

When God rested on the seventh day of creation, he didn't stop working. He didn't set things in motion and then sit down to simply observe all that would happen. What Jesus is saying is

---

God's working in the world doesn't depend on me; yet the God of the universe invites my participation.

---

that God has always been at work throughout history, and he will continue to work until the end of time. There's always a parade!

In the following verses, Jesus tells us what it is like to be in the parade: "The Son can do nothing by himself. He does only what he sees the Father doing, and in the same way. For the Father loves the Son, and tells him everything he is doing" (John 5:19-20). Henry Blackaby and Claude King describe Jesus' approach to God's activity:

> *The Father has been working right up until now.*
> *Now the Father has Me working.*
> *I do nothing on My own initiative.*
> *I watch to see what the Father is doing.*
> *I do what I see the Father already is doing.*
> *You see, the Father loves me.*
> *He shows Me everything that He, Himself, is doing.*[6]

If I want to join the parade, I must begin by recognizing that there really is a parade going by—and God wants me in it! Why? Because he loves me.

Truth #2: He Invites Us, As a Couple, to Join Him in His Work
There is no question that God invites us, individually, to join him in his work. But does he also invite us as a couple? Most certainly. How can we know that? By going back to the beginning. We've already noted that marriage was part of the original creation story.

6. Henry T. Blackaby and Claude V. King, *Experiencing God* (Nashville: Broadman and Holman, 1994), 48.

It was a part of what God did on the sixth day that pleased him very much.

Now use your imagination for a moment. Imagine Adam and Eve in the Garden of Eden, prior to the entrance of sin into the human experience. A major part of their life in the Garden was shared with God. There were daily visits when God would walk and talk with them in the cool of the day. How do you picture those visits? Did he walk with them as a couple? If we were to follow the emphasis of today's culture, we would imagine God coming into the Garden and first talking with Adam. Then when he had finished with Adam, he would go spend some time talking with Eve. And then he would leave. Sort of awkward, but it reflects our individualistic approach to spiritual growth and issues of spirituality. If we had a close friend who told us that he or she really cared about our marriage, and that friend always wanted to talk with us separately, we would be confused.

God cares about us, not just as individuals, but also as a couple. God is a relational God who cares deeply about the quality of our relationships. God created humans so that he could have a relationship with them. God created marriage so that we could have an intimate relationship with another person. If he cared about this in the original creation, then it follows that he would still care about our marriage relationship and want to be an intimate part of it.

God *invites* us. He takes the initiative. Since it is God who is doing the inviting, our response must be centered on what he is doing. We join a parade to participate in what is already planned and what is already taking place. That is a "parade-centered" attitude. That is a God-centered attitude, and that is to be our response to his invitation.

Truth #3: There Are a Variety of Ways We Can Participate.
I grew up in a church that had a strong missionary emphasis. We had missionaries speaking in our church on a regular basis.

I remember thinking as a young boy that only people who were involved in missions were really doing God's work. Perhaps those in full-time Christian work might also qualify, I thought, but they could never quite measure up to what the missionary could do.

Looking back, I see the foolishness of that attitude. There are many ways in which we can participate with God. The apostle Peter gives us insight into what it means to be spiritually intimate with God:

> *Do you want more and more of God's kindness and peace? Then learn to know him better and better. For as you know him better, he will give you, through his great power, everything you need for living a truly good life: he even shares his own glory and his own goodness with us! And by that same mighty power he has given us all the other rich and wonderful blessings he promised; for instance, the promise to save us from the lust and rottenness all around us, and to give us his own character.* 2 Pet. 1:2-4

Here Peter is affirming that the power to grow doesn't come from within us, but from God. God not only takes the initiative, but he also gives us his very own nature and character to help us as we participate with him in his activities. Peter continues with the "how":

> *But to obtain these gifts, you need more than faith; you must also work hard to be good, and even that is not enough. For then you must learn to know God better and discover what he wants you to do. Next, learn to put aside your own desires so that you will become patient and godly, gladly letting God have his way with you. This will make possible the next step, which is for you to enjoy other people and to like them, and*

finally you will grow to love them deeply. The more you go on in this way, the more you will grow strong spiritually and become fruitful and useful to our Lord Jesus Christ. 2 Pet. 1:5-8

Spiritual intimacy, or spirituality, is more than belief in certain facts. It must lead to action. And Peter tells us that we must work hard at these actions in order to know God better and to grow strong spiritually. If we are called to do this as a couple, then we must work hard together as a couple. But what do we do?

Over the centuries, the actions we can take to grow spiritually strong and intimate with God have been called the spiritual disciplines. Some people have approached these disciplines incorrectly, turning them into works that must be done in order to find God's favor. But if we look at them in light of what Peter has just said to us, we see that they are simply means of spiritual growth—they are ways in which we can participate with God. Dallas Willard reminds us that "to reject them wholesale is to insist that growth in the spirit is something that just happens all by itself." [7]

Others might say that spiritual growth does "just happen by itself" if we "eat spiritual food." By that they usually mean reading and studying the Bible; these are actually spiritual disciplines.

In chapters 5 through 16 we will describe twelve spiritual disciplines that couples can do together.

Truth #4: These Spiritual Disciplines Will Bring Us to Points of Crisis

Whenever we respond to God's invitation to join him in his work, something is going to have to change within us. Once we step off the curb and join the parade, life changes. We will come to forks in the road and will face some important choices that

7. Dallas Willard, *The Spirit of the Disciplines* (San Francisco: Harper, 1988), 153.

only we can make. And these choices are not made once and for all; they will be faced over and over again as the parade marches forward and we march along with it.

We will face two types of crises as we step off the curb. Let's look at these two crises and what they involve.

We must face our own fears and defensiveness. The early years of our marriage were filled with turmoil as we worked hard to iron out our differences, launch a career, and learn how to parent three boys. There wasn't much time left to develop any sense of spiritual intimacy together—at least that was our rationale for not doing anything. It wasn't that we didn't know it needed to be the foundation of our marriage; it was just too easy for us to use up our energy on other, more pressing problems. We made certain we spent time with our boys, teaching them spiritual principles and praying with them. But we never got around to developing spiritually together.

On the surface, one would think that at least praying together as husband and wife would have been easy for us, especially since I was a pastor during those earlier years. We both grew up in Christian homes and had learned early to pray with other people. I could pray in church services and meetings, or even with other people in my office. But praying with Jan presented a whole different experience for me—one that was threatening.

I came face-to-face with my own fears of being known, of being seen by Jan as less than she might be willing to tolerate. A whole bundle of fears rose up within me every time Jan suggested, or we heard someone else suggest, that we should be praying together as a couple.

Jan had always seemed ready and willing, leaving me to think it was my fears holding us back. I can't remember when, but I know that at some point years ago I decided to break through my fears of intimacy—or whatever else I was afraid of—and resolved to begin to pray with my wife. Of course, that was when Jan's fears rose to the surface. It was easy for her to want spiritual intimacy when she was the only one wanting it. When I was willing, it wasn't as easy for her as she thought.

As with any fear, once I faced it it shrank in size and no longer intimidated me. The crisis was over, at least at that stage. There have been other crises over the years. Fear of being rejected once someone got to know the "real" me would stir inside me, and I would find myself becoming resistive again. So the crisis isn't a once-for-all kind of thing. Our old fears sometimes come back to visit, even though they're disguised in different clothes.

We must adjust our priorities and activities. Henry Blackaby makes the point that "you can't stay where you are and go with God."[8] He goes through a list of people in the Bible who had to make changes in their lives when they responded to God's invitation. Beginning with Noah and continuing all the way to Saul, who even had his name changed to Paul, we can see that life will change when we step off the curb and join the parade.

"You can't stay where you are and go with God."

Perhaps one of the clearest pictures of the change required in following Jesus is found in the challenges Peter experienced when the Gentile Cornelius sent for him. God was already at work in Cornelius's life. He told Cornelius to send for Peter. But God had to prepare Peter for some very significant changes in his attitudes and behaviors. God prepared a vision for Peter, which not only challenged everything he believed about kosher foods but also opened up a whole new perspective regarding the "unclean" Gentiles. Peter went to see a man whose house, by standards of Jew-

8. Henry T. Blackaby and Claude V. King, *Experiencing God* (Nashville: Broadman and Holman, 1994), 147.

ish piety, Peter shouldn't have even entered. You see, God was already busy in Cornelius's life, and God invited Peter to join the parade and become part of the action. Later on, Peter told Cornelius about what God had challenged him to look at. The result led not only to Cornelius's conversion, but it also changed Peter's life and the whole course of the early church. (See Acts 10 for the complete story.)

Peter had to make some major adjustments, both in his attitudes and in his behaviors. We are called to make the same kinds of adjustments. Some of these adjustments may be major ones, like Peter's, or they may be less radical. But we can count on our lives shifting—and not feeling terribly comfortable at times—when we step off that curb.

Truth #5: The Resulting Deepening of Our Spiritual Intimacy Will Prepare Us for Our Future

Peter promises that "the more you go on in this way, the more you will grow strong spiritually" (2 Pet. 1:8). The goal of developing spiritual intimacy in our marriage prepares us as a couple for what lies ahead of us. Eugene H. Peterson wrote a book some years ago about the Psalms of Ascent. He titled the book *A Long Obedience in the Same Direction.* We are called as a couple to that kind of obedience. And it is the exercising of the spiritual disciplines that helps us to be obedient over the long haul.

Developing spiritual intimacy in our marriage prepares us as a couple for what lies ahead of us.

The experience of God at work in us as a couple will always call us to obedience. Our obedience is a response to God's love for us and is an expression of our love for him. As you read through this book, God will call you to be obedient. Not every discipline will apply to your marriage, but some will, and God will speak to your heart and say, "That's an important one for both of you to work on." Your obedience isn't to be out of duty or obligation; rather, it is to be a loving response to a loving God. That same loving response is what motivates you to respond to your husband or wife.

As we look back over the years of our own marriage, Jan and I can see how the spiritual disciplines have helped us live through what certainly felt like the dark nights of our souls—times when it seemed that all was lost, even our connection with God. David must have felt like this when Saul was chasing him. "Where is God?" he must have asked over and over again. "Why is everything going wrong?" would have been another viable question. Peter must have felt it as soon as the cock crowed the third time. In spite of all his best intentions, he had betrayed his Lord, and now Jesus was gone and there was no way to make things right.

For us, there were a number of years when we faced things within our family that made us wonder if we would survive, not just as a couple, but as parents and even as individuals. One of our children became deeply involved in drugs and turned his back on everything he had been taught and everything we believed. We wondered where God was and when he was going to keep his promises from Scripture that we were holding on to. During those "dark nights," we felt cut off from God and at many times at odds with each other.

Although our primary motivation for beginning to develop spiritual intimacy wasn't to keep evil happenings at bay, I'm not sure how we would have survived those years without the foundation those disciplines provided for us. We wanted to be obedient. It was our ability to come together to God and open ourselves up to him that sustained us, even when our feelings were crying out that all was hopeless.

Not every couple will go through the long dark nights, but

every couple will at least have some dark moments, and only the obedience of the disciplines will prepare you for those trying and challenging times.

We've identified the process. Before we look at how to get started, let's look first at some of the barriers we're going to encounter as we step off the curb together to join God in his work.

TO TALK ABOUT TOGETHER

- As you look at your present family, to what degree is it marriage centered as opposed to child centered?
- Discuss how you would answer if someone were to ask you, "In what ways is your marriage uniquely Christian?"
- What are you doing individually to develop the spiritual aspects of your life?
- What adjustments might you have to make if you begin to work on the spiritual disciplines as a couple? Time? Priorities? What are some fears you might face?
- If you've had some dark nights of the soul, what gave you the strength to stay and work on things together? How will developing spiritual intimacy in your marriage prepare you for any rough times that might be ahead?

Growing Together: *If It Was Easy, We'd Already Be Doing It*

OR several years while I was in junior high school, I had trouble sleeping. My legs ached. As long as I was on the move, I wasn't aware of any pain, but when I would lie down to go to sleep, I felt the pain. My parents dismissed my agony by saying, "Oh, it's probably just growing pains." Eventually I noticed a bump starting to develop on each leg just below my knees. When I showed my parents this change in the shape of my legs, they decided to take me to the doctor.

After an examination, the doctor took some X rays. When he came back into the room, he told us that I had Osgood Schlater's disease. Simply put, I had grown too fast, which caused the top of my shin bone to split. The ligaments on the front of my legs pulled part of the bone away, causing the lumps on my legs. The doctor assured me that when my rapid growth started to slow down, the aches and pains would ease. As we left the doctor's office, my dad said to me, "See, I told you they were growing pains." I still have those two bumps. Most of the time, they don't hurt anymore, mostly because my bone growth is fin-

ished. But every time I look at my knees, I'm reminded that growth can be painful.

I see this principle at work in people's emotional problems. Whether in my office or in the hospital, it's difficult for people to face some of the things that are destroying their ability to live a normal life. To someone outside the problem, the solution seems clear—just face the problem and move on. I've had people say this to themselves and then look at me and say, "Why can't I just do what I need to do and get on with it?" I'll often toss the question back to them, and after a few moments' reflection they respond, "I guess I don't want to go through the pain." Emotional growth can be even more painful than physical growth.

It is very clear that if we are going to develop spiritual intimacy in our marriage, whether we are just beginning or are adding to what we are already experiencing together spiritually, the very idea of growing—of doing more—suggests that we are about to press beyond our present capacity. And whenever we grow, or press forward, we are going to experience "growing pains." And who wants to hurt? Especially if it seems that they have a choice *not* to hurt.

SPIRITUAL INTIMACY IS ALWAYS INTENTIONAL

As a young boy, I could do nothing to slow down my physical growth. As long as I ate and slept, I would grow, and my knees would ache. But when it comes to the growth and development of spiritual intimacy, it will never happen unless we make a decision to make it happen. Spiritual intimacy is a part of our marriage relationship that we enter into through mutual obedience to the revelation of God in Jesus Christ. Obedience is always intentional; it involves making a choice.

It's not difficult for us to recognize and accept that, as individuals, we experience spiritual growth as we choose to be obedient and then carry out whatever helps our growth, such as reading the Bible, praying, and worshiping. Yet we think that spiritual intimacy in marriage will just come naturally as a result of our individual spiritual growth. That assumption prevents us from understanding the process of developing mutual spiritual intimacy. It never "just happens."

Why It Is So Difficult
You'd think everyone would want to choose to step off the curb and join the parade. Most Christian couples do, but they get discouraged at the first try. We are forgetting where we began—back in the Garden. We've already noted that when Adam and Eve sinned, everything changed. Their first response after eating the forbidden fruit was one of fear, guilt, and shame. And since that first episode in the Garden, we are all in the same condition. When the time comes for us to step off the curb, we begin to doubt whether or not we can, because we are filled with fears over what the future holds and with guilt and shame over our past. When it comes time for us to step off the curb as a couple, we are hindered by several other factors as well.

Male/Female Differences
The title of John Gray's book, *Men Are from Mars, Women Are from Venus,* says it all very succinctly. It's like we are from two different planets. Not only are there obvious, and pleasing, differences between men and women, but there are also a number of not-so-obvious differences that affect our ability to develop spiritual intimacy.

For starters, men tend to be "fixers," whereas women tend to be "relators." This seems to be an innate tendency, even going beyond culture. Several years ago, I was in Cambodia teaching basic counseling skills to a group of young pastors. We were working

27

on the skill of "listening," and I had divided them into groups of three to practice listening. One person was the counselor, another was the client with the problem, and the third person was an observer. After the exercise we discussed with the whole class each group's experience of listening. The women in the group said, "The men only listen a short time and then they want to fix the problem." And when the men spoke up, it was very clear that listening was difficult for them; they'd much rather find a quick solution.

So at the outset we have a problem: What can a man "fix" in order to develop spiritual intimacy? Nothing! Spiritual intimacy is part of relationship—and relating is something women tend to do more naturally and comfortably than men do. Perhaps that's why I've found in my years as a counselor that although both husbands and wives will agree that spiritual intimacy is important, it is usually the woman who best knows how to go about developing intimacy.

Another important difference is that when men feel fear, shame, or guilt, they usually want to go off by themselves and think about what they can do about the problem. When women feel fear, shame, or guilt, they will usually seek someone to talk to about what they are feeling. We can imagine what would have happened to Adam and Eve if God hadn't come to walk with them that evening. Adam would have tried to retreat to some quiet point in the Garden and Eve would have been looking for him—since there was no one else to talk to!

This scenario is repeated daily in our marriages. The man wants to retreat and think about a solution, while the woman seeks out someone with whom to talk. The woman is actually doing the work of intimacy. For the two essential ingredients for any kind of intimacy, including spiritual intimacy, are a willingness to share what is going on in one's life and a willingness to become vulnerable with the other person. Men tend to avoid both of these practices. This is why, with most of the couples I've talked with, it is the woman who is pressing for more intimacy.

The man wants to retreat and think about a solution,
while the woman seeks out someone to talk with.

When we look at Ephesians 5, we see another difficulty between men and women. What is it that a wife needs, and what is it that a husband needs? Paul tells us when he writes, "A man must love his wife as a part of himself; and the wife must see to it that she deeply respects her husband—obeying, praising, and honoring him" (Eph. 5:33). Paul is defining what motivates us within our marriage relationship. Although we are speaking in general terms, it is safe to say that a woman is most motivated by knowing she is loved, and a man is most motivated by knowing he is respected. Of course, both marriage partners need both love and respect, but what motivates them most will affect how each of them approaches spiritual intimacy.

Am I saying that men simply are not designed for intimacy? Certainly not. But, in most marriages, the woman's inclinations toward relationship and giving and receiving love urge her toward the quest of spiritual intimacy, while the man will tend toward problem solving and withdrawal, and his need for respect can render him less willing to be vulnerable and honest about his fears and failings. When mutual spiritual growth becomes a goal, we need to recognize that these differences will sometimes work against the process.

Personality Differences
The gender differences between men and women appear simple when compared to our personality differences.

My own marriage offers a perfect example of this. My wife, Jan, is a people person. Interaction with others energizes her. When I first met her, I admired her ability to interact with almost everyone. In college, she was involved in different committees and activities, and I enjoyed watching from a distance. I, however, am not a people person; interaction drains energy from me, and I need times of solitude in order to refuel. After Jan and I married, gradually my need for solitude became very boring to her, while her need for constant interaction created chaos for me. Our individual tasks were obvious—change each other to be more like "me"!

---

*My need for solitude became boring to her;
her need for constant interaction
created chaos for me.*

From a distance, we can all agree that the differences in our personalities add variety to our lives. But something strange happens once we get married. We marry someone whose personality differs to some degree from ours—opposites do attract. But once we are married to someone different from us, those opposite traits, previously so attractive to us, now become areas in need of change. At heart, we really want our mate to be more like us. So we set out on a frustrating course of action to attempt to do the impossible.

Why is it that what was once so attractive now needs to be modified? It goes back to the Garden. Because sin entered the human experience, we bring fear into every relationship, especially marriage. We are basically afraid that the other person will begin to find some fault in us and leave us. What better way to remove this fear than to make the other person into a carbon copy of ourself. Then what can they dislike and reject about us? Nothing, for we are the same.

But what happens if those characteristics that attracted us to the other person are suppressed or modified? If we were actually able to change the other person into our own image, we would then become even more fearful of rejection and abandonment, for then they would know even more intimately all of the weaknesses and failings of our particular personality.

Different Approaches to Our Relationship with God

When we approach the subject of spiritual intimacy, our personality differences obviously predispose us to certain approaches to God, to worship, to service, and to our basic understanding of how religion relates to life. In the creation of the Bible, God inspired a number of writers, all having their own unique personalities. This is why some books of the Bible are more personal to us than others; we identify more closely with some writers.

Perhaps you've already had some experience like this with your spouse. He thinks the apostle Paul is the epitome of what every man in Christ should be like. He is strong in his faith, driven to serve the Lord, and able to interact intellectually with the great minds of his age. She thinks the apostle Paul is a workaholic who is always meddling in other people's lives. She prefers the apostle Peter as a model. After all, he is so spontaneous and open to what is going on around him. Peter isn't driven like the apostle Paul is. Her husband thinks Peter is something of a flake. He can't be depended on when the chips are down. And on and on the argument can continue. What is really being "discussed" here is this: What form will the expression of our spiritual intimacy take—mine or his/hers?

When we look at the personalities of the early apostles, we can see great diversity. Paul was always looking over the edge at what was coming. It was his teaching and leadership that helped the early Christians break free from the shackles of the Mosaic law. Wherever he went he was a catalyst for people coming to Jesus and then coming together to form a church. His concerns about the future kept him in touch with these young churches as he helped to draw them closer together and closer to their newfound Lord.

James, the brother of Jesus, was always pulling the disciples back to a sense of duty and responsibility. What was one to do as a follower of Jesus Christ? He believed the traditions of the past needed to be integrated into the present.

John, the beloved disciple, articulated fresh new ideas about what it meant to follow Jesus. He was an early mystic and was able to not only present important concepts about Jesus, such as Jesus' words, "I am the Way—yes, and the Truth, and the Life," and "I am the Bread of Life," but also to pull us into the future to give us a vision of what the end times would be like.

And then there was Peter, the man of action. He was the problem solver. During the council of Jerusalem, it was Peter who brought together Paul and James, along with their followers, bringing peace between these opposing schools of thought about the early church's mission (see Acts 15). Peter later got himself in trouble with Paul when, in trying to keep everyone happy, he ended up offending the early Gentile believers. But like most problem solvers, when confronted with something he was doing wrong, he listened and "fixed the problem," even if it was within himself.

We can describe these four "spiritual personalities" as: (1) the Visionary; (2) the Traditionalist; (3) the Catalyst; and (4) the Problem Solver. One of these approaches to the faith will be similar to our own.

The Visionary is always looking beyond. He or she is trying to see the overall picture and won't rest until everything somehow fits into some large plan. Past, present, and future all fit together to make a whole, but it is the future that leads through the present. If you are this type of person, your approach to spiritual intimacy can easily be sidetracked as you work hard at "doing things right." Resistance will often take the form of questioning whether or not you have found the best way to approach this whole spiritual intimacy issue. As you discuss the various approaches available, you can easily lose sight of spiritual intimacy as the objective because you enjoy the intellectual stimulation of the broader discussion.

The Traditionalist has a strong sense of duty and tradition. For this person, the way to do things is the way they have always been done, only a little better. Routines that have lost their meaning to others are often still meaningful for the traditionalist. When change in routine is suggested, the traditionalist often feels threatened and insecure. If you are the traditionalist, you will be wary of doing anything that is new and different as you focus on developing spiritual intimacy within your marriage. Your spouse may feel that you are always dragging your feet.

The Catalyst is always concerned about people. Since this person is checking to be sure that everyone is feeling OK, it would seem that this type of person would be wide open to the quest for spiritual intimacy. To them, everything is relational. No one works alone. In fact, they are always working on building a unified team, whether it's at work or within their family. If you are this type of person, you may get so involved with others that you neglect the spiritual needs of your own marriage or simply find that you don't have the time or energy to address them.

The Problem Solver approaches spiritual intimacy as a course of action. "Great," he says, "let's just do it!" If we stop to discuss how we might develop spiritual intimacy, problem solvers will often lose interest, for they don't like being told "how" to do anything. They especially don't like to discuss the "how"—just tell them what to do and they will figure out the "how" as they go along. They are often very involved for a short time, working on some particular part of spiritual intimacy. But once that is accomplished, it's on to something else. The ongoing development of spiritual intimacy can be experienced as confining—it's far more exciting to start something new than to maintain and improve something they're already doing.

Fear and Resistance

It is easy to see that when we add these different personalities to our differences as male and female, we have a number of barriers to embarking on this journey of marital spiritual intimacy. It's clear why this kind of growth eludes so many couples. We need to realize, also, that our differences tap right into our fears.

Spiritual intimacy is based on obedience to the Lord and submission not only to him but to each other. This obedient, submissive spirit is demonstrated through vulnerability and mutual sharing of the heart. One may obey out of fear, and one may submit out of fear, but one will never allow oneself to be vulnerable out of fear. In fact, fear will destroy any sense of vulnerability and shut down any possibility of sharing from the heart.

---

*One may obey out of fear or submit out of fear,
but one will never allow oneself to be
vulnerable out of fear.*

But our fears are often hidden, even from ourselves. We have three basic strategies for coping with our fears. These strategies are connected to the three basic movements of our emotions: movement toward, movement against, and movement away from others.[1] How do our fears and the way we cope with them affect our spiritual growth in marriage?

Fears will push us toward someone in the wrong way, rather than move us toward that person in love. Usually we move toward another person through friendship; we move toward those people

1. For a discussion of these three movements of our emotions, see David Stoop, *Self-Talk, Key to Personal Growth*, revised edition (Grand Rapids: Baker/Fleming Revell, 1982, 1996).

we love and trust. But when fear enters the picture, the resulting insecurity will lead us into behavior that actually works against the intimacy we want. For instance, we can try to cover up insecurity with perfectionism. A couple talks together about developing a closer relationship with God and about doing this together. They really want this. But fear invades the desire, creating thoughts like, *We must become "better"*—better persons or better Christians—before we can really get serious about our search for intimacy. Or we say to ourselves, "I think I must be further down the road of perfection as an individual before we can ever do anything together."

Our perfectionism will often exaggerate our personality styles, causing the visionary to become even more analytical, the traditionalist to strive to be even more disciplined, the catalyst to be driven more to help others, or the problem solver to actually create some new problems to be solved. In other words, when fear enters into our movement toward spiritual intimacy, we tend to fall back on what we do well already. This kind of perfectionism can create any number of other things we need to improve before we can get serious about actually working on spiritual intimacy in our marriage.

On the surface, it appears as if the perfectionist is moving in the right direction, but underneath, fear and insecurity reign. We can begin to diminish its effect on us only in a context of security and unconditional acceptance. Only when we have broken the power of perfectionism can we discover the freedom to "come boldly to the very throne of God and stay there to receive his mercy and to find grace to help us in our times of need" (Heb. 4:16).

Fears will push us against the other person, often through anger and hostility. In the area of spiritual growth and intimacy, our anger or hostility usually isn't overt; it tends to be much more subtle.

35

We may hold a grudge, for instance. I remember one husband, Pete, saying to me that he couldn't pray with his wife because he was still angry with her over something that had happened years before. When I asked if he had talked about his anger with his wife, Jennifer, he said, "No, it doesn't do any good. She can't understand why I feel the way I do." When I turned to Jennifer, she was crying softly. She didn't know whether to be angry or sad as she said to me, "I can't believe he's saying that. We've talked about it a number of times, and he always seems satisfied with my apology. But then every time we start to talk about something he doesn't want to do, he goes back and brings up that old story again."

After talking with them for some time, it was obvious that Pete was holding on to his hostility as a protection against having to do something that was frightening for him. As long as he wasn't challenged to step out and take a risk in their relationship together, the hostility was buried. But if something came up that stirred up those inner fears, out came the hostility—and that was the end of the discussion.

If talk about intimacy, especially spiritual intimacy, is threatening or frightening to me, I push it away with my anger. Pete wasn't stomping around; his anger appeared more as hurt over a past event. But the hurt was long since buried beneath his grudge and now served the same purpose as open hostility: It kept him away from what he may have longed for, but what he also feared.

Sometimes fear moves us against the other person through general irritability. Have you noticed how easy it is to focus on some irritating behavior in your spouse just when the two of you are trying to work on spiritual intimacy? Whenever the subject comes up, there's a feeling of restlessness; we can't sit still and talk, and we experience a general sense of anger or resentment that we can't attach to anything specific. This overall feeling of dis-ease is another way that fear interrupts many couples' progress.

Fears will move us away from others. Perhaps the best illustration of this behavior is withdrawal, emotional or physical. We just shut down. Someone has described this as "pulling the blinds down within our eyes." You've been on the receiving end of this when you are talking with someone and suddenly realize he isn't really there anymore. You can tell by the blank look in his eyes. Inside, he has "run away" from you, or he has "pulled the blinds" behind his eyes and shut you out.

Busyness is one of the most common ways we can withdraw from another person. One of the things that Jennifer did in response to Pete's hostility was to get busy. She had the most organized house in the neighborhood, for she often stayed up late at night working on some project. She kept complete files on everything that had ever happened in their family. Every room in her home was carefully organized, and it required a great amount of time for her to maintain that sense of order.

Often, following an argument with Pete over his long-held hurt, Jennifer would reorganize some part of the house. This would keep her working until late at night, long after Pete had gone to sleep. If he was aware enough to say to her, "Jenn, you're ignoring me," she would innocently reply, "No, Pete, this is something I've been putting off and need to finish." And even though Pete would be right, Jennifer's busyness was a form of withdrawal that was difficult to penetrate.

Often the person using busyness as a means of withdrawal will be busy at the office. He or she may agree that they need to spend some time together to talk about spiritual intimacy, but when it comes down to actually scheduling that time together, it is impossible—too busy!

Silence can be a very frustrating form of withdrawal. When one partner shuts down and is silent, the other partner often presses for a response. Emotions rise, and soon the silence is broken by an angry outburst, followed by one or both leaving the room. A common form of silence is achieved by becoming "lost" in some TV program. Even the commercials get in the way of a response to the partner.

A FRIGHTENING QUESTION

As you've been reading this chapter, perhaps one big question has been lurking in your mind: What if I'm the only one in this marriage who's interested in spiritual intimacy?

What if I'm the only one in this marriage who's interested in spiritual intimacy?

This is an important question. But let's reflect on the barriers we've already mentioned, especially those related to fear. When it appears to you that you are the only one wanting to develop spiritual intimacy in the marriage, it is difficult to see that the real issue may be your spouse's fear. What we see is not always what is really going on inside the other person.

For example, if your husband gets angry with you when you bring up the subject of spirituality, recognize that perhaps he has chosen the path of hostility to cover up his fear. Or if your wife withdraws from you and you feel rejected and ignored, you need to see that the withdrawal is not an expression of rejection, but of fear. It is so important—probably the most important point in this chapter—that we see our partner's fear, because our response to fear is going to be much different than our response to hostility or rejection.

But you say, "She really is angry with me" or "He really is rejecting me!" Are you certain? Why not check it out? Ask, "I can sense that you don't really want to talk about this right now. Is it because you are uncomfortable [another word for fear] with what we are talking about?" Or, "I know you are angry with me right now, but are you also uncomfortable talking about this?" When you can make that distinction, both of you can respond differently.

When you feel that you are the only one in the marriage who is interested in spiritual intimacy, it is important for you to remember the apostle Peter's words. Even though he is writing to wives, the principle is the same for both husbands and wives: "Wives, fit in with your husbands' plans; for then if they refuse to listen when you talk to them about the Lord, they will be won by your respectful, pure behavior. Your godly lives will speak to them better than any words" (1 Pet. 3:1-2).

I recall something Jan said to me one time when we were not doing well with each other. She said, "You go ahead and do what you want, but I'm going to work more on being God's woman." And that was all she said about the subject. Now, on the surface that may seem to have been manipulative or hostile, but it wasn't. The key is to make the statement once, clearly, and then win the other person over by your silence and godly behavior. Take the time to work on your own relationship with the Lord, and entrust your spouse's participation to God.

So How Can We Begin?

We've looked at a number of barriers to developing spiritual intimacy in marriage. Most of what we have described is simply a part of every marriage. So the natural question is, Given these barriers, how do we begin? Perhaps a more specific question is, How do we use this book to begin?

1. Start small. Sometimes we feel that when we have grown so much as an individual it is a simple step to bring all of that spiritual maturity into our marriage. But when we make the attempt, we fall flat on our face. In so doing, we not only experience the difficulty of working together on spiritual intimacy, but we also suffer a major setback in our personal walk with the Lord. So start with lowered expectations.

This book is a good beginning. Agree to read it together. Perhaps each of you will want your own copy, or you can read the same copy and use different colored markers to highlight what is especially meaningful to you. You might want to wait until each of you has finished the book before you begin to talk about your responses. It might even be helpful if you read and discuss the whole book before you begin any of the specific spiritual disciplines described in the next section.

2. *Talk about your fears.* Your specific fears may not have been mentioned in this chapter. We certainly haven't listed all of them. But you should remember one principle where fear is concerned: Whenever we try to ignore our fears, they grow bigger until they eventually become monsters in our lives. When we can bring them out into the light and talk about them, they grow smaller and we begin to feel that we can tackle whatever it is we've been avoiding.

Talking is not necessarily the major task in communicating; many of us are very good at putting our thoughts and feelings into words. But listening is the skill that will really pay off. It is especially important to listen to what the other person is really saying when the topic is fear. When your partner describes one of his or her fears, try to repeat what has just been said—in your own words—until both of you are sure that you know what he or she is saying. It is amazing how communication can improve when we focus more on listening than on talking.

You also need to remember that you can't "fix" a feeling. If one of you tries to fix the other's feeling of fear, you will only add to the fear—and also instill a sense of shame in the other person for feeling the fear in the first place. All you need to do is listen and let the other person know that you have heard and understood.

3. Use the questions. After you have finished the whole book and talked about the different parts of it that each of you highlighted, go back and take it a chapter at a time—perhaps one chapter a week. Discuss the questions provided at the end of each chapter. These questions are designed to help you overcome some of the barriers we've described in this chapter. Reveal only what you are comfortable revealing, and don't feel pressure to move too quickly. Of course, you have to press beyond your comfort zone, but don't go too far at first or you will only add to your fear and resistance and make the whole process seem too difficult.

The process of spiritual intimacy within marriage is grounded in a common obedience to God, who must become our focus. I, my spouse, and Jesus Christ are meeting together. This communion with God as a couple is our goal. So don't rush the process. Just enjoy being together.

TO TALK ABOUT TOGETHER

- Which personality—Visionary, Traditionalist, Catalyst, Problem Solver—can you relate to the most? How does it color your relationship with God?
- What is your biggest fear as you begin to develop spiritual intimacy in your marriage? What is your spouse's biggest fear? How might each of you avoid triggering the other's fear or focus on dealing with the fear, should you happen to trigger it? How can you plan to deal with fear?
- Describe some small steps for developing spiritual intimacy that would be comfortable for you but that would also stretch your comfort zone.

THREE

When Two Become One:
What's the Spiritual Connection?

BOB and Andrea were typical of many couples who finally come to a counselor. After years of struggling with each other, neither one of them appeared to have any real commitment to the marriage, and even though they wouldn't admit it, their motive for seeking counseling seemed to be the desire to be able to say later, "We tried everything—even counseling—and nothing worked! So we got a divorce." As we talked together, neither of them expressed any sense of the "us" in their marriage. When I asked them about that, they didn't really know how to respond; they were each too busy thinking about the "me." Both Bob and Andrea said several times, "I don't really believe in divorce, but . . ." and then finished with a variety of statements, each of which emphasized how "God couldn't possibly want *me* to be unhappy." Years ago they had stopped thinking about who they were as a couple and why God had brought them together.

CHRISTIAN ANSWERS TO *WHO? WHY?* AND *HOW?*

Like Bob and Andrea, each one of us needs to answer two basic questions, not only in the course of our marriages but in the course of all we do and strive to become. The first: *Who* are we? The second logically follows: *Why* are we? This culture that inclines people so easily toward divorce has adopted the view, whether consciously or not, that we are who we are by no particular plan or purpose. We are here simply because the evolutionary process led to "me" and to "you." And since we are here only by chance, the "why" of our existence is to "eat, drink, and be merry" or—more simply put—to be happy. Sometimes we arrive at a somewhat nobler purpose—to be a success or to make a positive contribution to society.

What we see in this attitude, which is so pervasive in our society, is a commitment to individual fulfillment. Our focus on individual happiness leads quite naturally to divorce, because it abandons the "we." And in order to buy into the divorce-centered responses to the *who* and *why* questions, we must effectively rule out God, or at least make God into some peripheral being who is only important in a very compartmental way within us. To many of us, God has become so marginal that issues related to him become important only as we approach the end of our life.

Much of what we've discussed in the earlier chapters is our answer to the question: "Who are we?" We believe we are a couple, created in the image of God, joined together in Christian marriage. We are called to be God's children—together.

We've also considered an important answer to the question: "Why are we together?" We are called together in this marriage in order to get to know God better. What makes a marriage distinctly Christian is the fulfillment of the answer to this question, which says that we, *together*, seek to develop a close, intimate relationship with God, the one who made us and wants to be an intimate part of our lives.

We now come to the third great question of life: "How are we to live?" With marital spiritual intimacy in mind, I've rephrased the question: "How do we live together in such a way that we can both come to know God better?" What can we do together, or what exercises can we both experience, in order to build spiritual intimacy within our marriage?

IS THAT ALL THERE IS?

As a young student in Bible college, I remember asking the college president, a saintly old man, how I could experience a more intimate relationship with God. Not being married at the time, I was asking for myself as an individual. When I told him that I was reading my Bible and praying, he asked me how often and for how long. When I answered, he simply and sincerely said, "You need to do more." But the "more" was more of the same— more prayer and more Bible study. These were the only identified ways, along with attending church and Sunday school, that one developed spiritual intimacy. And much of what I experienced at that time in church and Sunday school was designed to help me study the Bible more.

While there is nothing wrong with prayer and Bible study, I had hoped, when I questioned my professor, that he would have something more for me. Were there no other ways to experience God? If I had been knowledgeable enough to ask him about spiritual disciplines such as solitude, fasting, or the Sabbath rest, he would probably have told me to be careful, for many who practice such things do so thinking they will somehow "earn their way" into heaven. And his attitude would have been characteristic of the teaching of that day in that setting. Today many Christians still hold the view that anything outside of prayer and

Bible study is questionable and that those who practice "disciplines" are trying to earn merits with God.

I had hoped that he would have something more
for me. Were there no other ways
to experience God?

Dangers of Disciplines

These fears have some foundation. A quick look into the book of Isaiah tells the story of abused disciplines; it didn't take long for God's people to miss the whole point of feasts, fasts, and sacrifices. The prophet cries out:

> *Shout with the voice of a trumpet blast; tell my people of their sins! Yet they act so pious! They come to the Temple every day and are so delighted to hear the reading of my laws—just as though they would obey them—just as though they don't despise the commandments of their God! How anxious they are to worship correctly; oh, how they love the Temple services!*
>
> *"We have fasted before you," they say. "Why aren't you impressed? Why don't you see our sacrifices? Why don't you hear our prayers? We have done much penance, and you don't even notice it!" I'll tell you why! Because you are living in evil pleasure even while you are fasting, and you keep right on oppressing your workers.* Isaiah 58:1-3

The people were surprised and offended when Isaiah called them to account for their lack of obedience. After all, they had been doing the right things. But their hearts were not involved. They were only going through the motions, seeing their "holy acts" as ways of winning God's favor.

This attitude continued on into the New Testament era. Dallas Willard notes that "no one who has looked squarely at the life of Jesus and the apostles can imagine them engaging in the strange behavior of a Macarius of Alexandria, or a Serapion, or a Pachomius: eating no cooked food for seven years, exposing the naked body to poisonous flies while sleeping in a marsh for six months, not lying down to sleep for forty or fifty years, not speaking a word for many years."[1] The list goes on and could include examples of people today who depend on rituals or who handle poisonous snakes. Any spiritual activity is abused when it becomes an end in itself, rather than a means of inviting God into our lives and seeking to understand and know him more intimately. Disciplines stop achieving what we want when we begin to depend on them as a way to get God's favor. God's favor comes to us through grace, not works (Eph. 2:8-9).

Disciplines stop achieving what we want when we begin to depend on them as a way to get God's favor.

How should we think of spiritual disciplines? A discipline is something we can do that will help us develop spiritual intimacy—with God and with each other. As Willard says, "A discipline for the spiritual life is, when the dust of history is blown away, nothing but an activity undertaken to bring us into a more effective cooperation with Christ and his Kingdom."[2] Disciplines are what Paul describes when he writes to Timothy, "Spend your time and energy in the exercise of keeping spiritually fit" (1 Tim. 4:7). Once we "step off the curb," disciplines are what we can do to participate in God's parade. And when we do them as a couple,

1. Dallas Willard, *The Spirit of the Disciplines* (San Francisco: Harper, 1988), 142.
2. Ibid., 156.

they lead to spiritual intimacy within our marriage. They are keys to life beyond "me."

ADDING ON, TAKING OFF

As we begin to look at specific spiritual disciplines, two general categories come into view. One includes disciplines of *abstaining from,* and the other, disciplines of *adding to.*

The disciplines of abstaining can be described by Paul's words, "mortify the deeds of the body" (Rom. 8:13, KJV). *Mortify* is a word that means "to put to the death." Matthew uses this same word to describe Jesus being put to death on the cross (see Matt. 26:59 and 27:1).

Paul also describes abstaining with the phrase "putting off" or "taking off." In Colossians 3:9 (NIV), Paul says, "Do not lie to each other, since you have *taken off* your old self with its practices" (italics added). Peter describes the same thing, but puts it like this: "Dear brothers, you are only visitors here. Since your real home is in heaven, I beg you to *keep away from* the evil pleasures of this world; they are not for you, for they fight against your very souls" (1 Pet. 2:11, italics added). So *putting to death, putting off, taking off,* or *keeping away from* are all phrases that describe one type of spiritual discipline. In another sense, these disciplines can be thought of as "breathing out," for when we breathe out, we rid our body of toxic substances, the behaviors and thoughts that are destructive to us and to others.

The other type of spiritual discipline is the opposite of the first, and it involves taking positive action by *adding to* or *putting on* something. In Ephesians 6, Paul tells us to *"put on* all of God's armor so that you will be able to stand safe against all strategies and tricks of Satan" (verse 11, italics added). In Colossians, Paul continues his "putting on" injunction by telling us to *"put on* the new self, which is being renewed in knowledge in the image of its Creator"

(Col. 3:10, NIV, italics added). In Romans 13:12, Paul urges us to not only *put off,* or "quit the evil deeds of darkness" but also to *"put on* the armor of right living, as we who live in the daylight should!" (italics added). In another sense, we can think of these disciplines as "breathing in" and bringing into our body healthy elements that are necessary for life. Just as we need to breathe in and out physically, there is a spiritual rhythm and pattern of putting on and putting off—putting off those things that harm us spiritually, and putting on those things that add to spiritual health.

There is nothing particularly mysterious about this on/off, in/out process. Unfortunately, we've heard more about "breathing in/breathing out" in discussions of Eastern religions than in our teachings about Christian faith. The reason this in/out principal shows up in other religions is that—it's true! Putting on and putting off are natural parts of spiritual growth; they always have been and continue to be so.

AN OVERVIEW OF SPIRITUAL HELPS

Each of the two major categories of spiritual disciplines breaks down into two smaller sets. Some disciplines focus primarily on the inner life, what happens inside of us; others focus primarily on the outer life, how we relate to others. The twelve disciplines we are going to consider can be listed like this:

"PUTTING ON"	"PUTTING OFF"
Focused on the inner life:	**Focused on the inner life:**
Prayer	Confession
Study/Meditation	Forgiveness
Submission	Giving
Focused on the outer life:	**Focused on the outer life:**
Worship	Solitude/Silence
Celebration	Fasting
Service	Sabbath Rest

This list is by no means exhaustive. These are the disciplines Jan and I are seeking to develop in our own marriage. If there are others you find helpful, add them to your list. They appear in many combinations and with various explanations in literature dating back to the days of the early church. We'll look first at the "putting on" disciplines of positive action; then we'll explore the "putting off" disciplines of getting rid of the negative, sinful actions in our lives.

You might already be practicing some of these spiritual activities—individually. But our goal is to discover how they can be practiced as a couple.

Spiritual intimacy in marriage means that we develop a *shared inner life.* "Putting on" disciplines that focus on our inner life together are prayer, study/meditation, and submission, covered in chapters 4, 5, and 6.

Spiritual intimacy in marriage means that
we develop a shared inner life.

Chapters 7, 8, and 9 will look at the three "putting on" disciplines connected to our shared outer life. These disciplines add to our shared intimacy, but are practiced among others—they are spiritual activities we do in the spiritual community of faith: worship, celebration, and service.

Chapters 10, 11, and 12 explore the three "putting off" disciplines connected to our shared inner life. These are the disciplines of confession, forgiveness, and giving.

Finally, chapters 13, 14, and 15 will look at the three "putting off" disciplines connected to our shared outer life. These will be the disciplines of solitude/silence, fasting, and Sabbath rest.

FOLLOWING IN JESUS' STEPS—TOGETHER

Why revisit old—some of them almost forgotten—*spiritual disciplines?* Are they just more "things" to tack on to an already loaded-down married life? Can a marriage that's already struggling bear the added responsibility of learning another spiritual "thing"?

Jan's and my experience, and the experience of the many couples we have counseled and watched, tells us that, not only can a struggling marriage bear more "spiritual" things, but these disciplines can add the new life that's needed to keep the relationship intact and help it to thrive. Old disciplines keep getting rediscovered by the Christian community *because they work.*

---

*These disciplines can add the new life that's needed
to keep the relationship intact
and help it to thrive.*

Jesus is our perfect picture of the balanced, thriving spiritual life. He truly "breathed in and out." He prayed, studied, meditated, and submitted to God's will. He confessed and forgave; he gave, worshiped, celebrated, and served. He spent time in solitude, he fasted, he took his Sabbath rest. We can follow in his footsteps. And the exciting thing is, we can follow him—as two who have "become one"—in the wonderful life that God meant marriage to be.

TO TALK ABOUT TOGETHER
- What have been some of the attitudes you have heard expressed over the years regarding spiritual disciplines? Which have influenced you the most?

- Describe ways you "put on" some things you want in your marriage and ways you "put off" the things you don't want in your marriage.
- Discuss some of the things you have done to make your marriage more "Christian."

FOUR

Praying Together:
Why Is It So Difficult?

I REMEMBER asking Andrea if she and Bob had ever prayed together. It was like setting a match to a firecracker. First she exploded, telling me how many times she had tried to get Bob to pray with her and how every time she tried it would end in a vicious argument. When I looked at Bob, he responded with his own explosion. He narrowed his eyes and snapped back at her, "I tried it once long ago, and all you did was preach at me in your prayer. I decided then and there that I would never try again! And I never did!"

"WHY CAN'T WE PRAY TOGETHER?"

We were speaking on the subject of spiritual intimacy in marriage at a convention recently, and someone in the audience commented on some statistics they had heard that reported that only 4 percent of Christian couples actually pray together. The audience generally agreed with those statistics. From my experience as a counselor and as a pastor, the 4 percent estimate, unfortunately, rings true.

Why is it so difficult to pray together as a married couple? There are several reasons.

A Difference in Expectations

Often, our expectations about praying together are very different from our spouse's. You may like to pray at a certain time every day. You're awake a moment before the alarm goes off, and that is when you like to read your Bible and pray. Your morning routine is always the same, and you can time it by the clock. If you're not a morning person, then you have another set time every day when you have your devotions. You like structure and schedule.

It's amazing how often someone who is very structured ends up married to someone who loves spontaneity. This type of person may like to have their prayer time while they exercise. Or perhaps they like to pray while in the shower, or in the car driving to work. After some attempts to coordinate times to pray together, both people begin to back away from the subject because, to them, what the other person wants just doesn't seem "natural" or spiritual enough. You stop talking about it together, and the problem becomes overwhelming. Eventually you just don't bring it up anymore. Or when you do talk, the guilt each one feels is enough to short-circuit the conversation.

If your expectations are very different from your spouse's, try this: First, talk about your feelings about prayer until you can agree that praying together is something you both want in your marriage. Then divide the responsibilities involved for how you will pray together. Perhaps the more structured person can take the responsibility for making certain you pray with each other each day, but the more spontaneous person is responsible for when and where you will pray together. If you can see that the other person's style is part of their personality and not some judgment of your style, you will find it easier to compromise with each other.

Prayer Is Very Disarming

I may be listening to a friend describe some difficult problem he or she is facing. It's much simpler for me to say, "I'll pray for you," as opposed to saying, "Let's pray together right now about this."

When I say that I'll pray, not so much is demanded of me. That doesn't mean my statement is meaningless or a means of avoiding my friend's problems. It simply means that I don't have to get too involved or become vulnerable. But if, at the end of the conversation, I offer to pray then and there, I'm involved. I'm offering much more of myself to a person when I invite him to hear my conversation with God. I am, in a good way, putting my spirituality on display, and that's not easy, even between marriage partners.

Praying Exposes the Quality of Our Relationship

Praying exposes, among other things, the level of intimacy in a relationship. If I say, "Let's pray together about this," I am demonstrating a degree of comfort and ease I feel in the relationship. But if I am uncomfortable saying it, I'm revealing an area of our relationship that isn't well developed yet. My discomfort with the idea of praying with this person may tell me more than I want to know about our friendship.

If I am uncomfortable praying with my spouse, that means I am uncomfortable with some part of our relationship. For instance, am I afraid a certain subject may come up in the prayer, and I don't want to approach that subject? Or do I feel that I am in some way spiritually inferior or superior to my partner, and I don't know how to handle that? If I can avoid the issue of praying together, I can also avoid whatever discomfort it is that I'm feeling about our relationship.

*If I am uncomfortable praying with my spouse,
that means I am uncomfortable with
some part of our relationship.*

Prayer Is Spiritual Warfare

We need to see prayer for what it is—it is an important part of spiritual warfare. It is one of the weapons we have as we battle "persons without bodies—the evil rulers of the unseen world, those mighty satanic beings and great evil princes of darkness who rule this world" (Eph. 6:12). Following this description of our enemy, Paul encourages us to "use every piece of God's armor to resist the enemy" (verse 13), and finishes that passage by urging us to "pray all the time" (verse 18).

*Whenever we pray, we are taking on the
enemy of our soul; we will
face some resistance.*

Whenever we pray, we are taking on the enemy of our soul. Prayer, along with all the other disciplines described in this book, is one of the primary weapons available to us as we enter the battle. To pray together is not just a simple activity we add to our day; it is an act of aggression against spiritual forces—and the enemy will resist us. As you work at praying together, realize that some of the difficulty you experience is due to this invisible spiritual battle. But be encouraged by the knowledge that you are entering into God's unseen activity, which is going on all around us!

✝ MAKING PRAYER A VITAL PART OF
LIFE TOGETHER

So what can we do, now that we know why prayer is
so difficult? Here are seven ways you and your spouse can begin
to pray together. They are described in order, from the easiest to
the more difficult. Begin where you are comfortable, and then
seek to work toward the more difficult over time. If you are already praying together, look them over to see if there are additional ways you can enjoy this discipline together.

1. Pray for each other. You can begin by praying for each other.
The Bible doesn't say directly, "Husbands and wives, pray for
each other." But it does say in James 5:16 that we all are to "pray
for each other so that you may be healed." One of the things Jan
and I do is find different prayers in the Bible and then agree to
pray them for each other. For example, Paul tells us how he prays
for the Philippians (see Phil. 1:9-10). We've found this prayer to
be a beautiful expression of what we want to experience together.
In fact, we often use this prayer of Paul's as our theme prayer for
couples' retreats. Pray this for your mate:

> *And this is my prayer: that your love may abound more and*
> *more in knowledge and depth of insight, so that you may be*
> *able to discern what is best and may be pure and blameless un-*
> *til the day of Christ.* Phil. 1:9-10 (NIV)

Read through Paul's letters and note his prayers. They can be a
very meaningful way for you to pray for each other. If you are
just beginning this discipline together, it is important that you
talk about what you are doing. Simply tell your spouse that you
are praying for him or her and that you are using Paul's prayer as
your prayer. Identify the passage you are using so that your
spouse can look it up and know what you are praying. You might

also use Ephesians 1:18-20, or Romans 15:5-6, or any other prayer you find in the Bible that expresses your heart. Don't be afraid to edit them a little to make them more personal.

The first step may not exactly make you feel like you are praying together, but it is a good place to begin if you are not yet praying together as a couple. It is also important to keep doing this step, even after you have added some of the other ways of praying together.

2. Pray silently—together. When couples are struggling with how to pray together and they want to begin, I often tell them to start this way. Take some time alone together and begin to talk about some of your concerns. As you finish the conversation, one of you may say to the other, "Let's pray about this."

Then have a time of silent prayer together. As you pray, you may want to hold hands as a reminder that, even though you are praying silently, you are praying together. When you finish, say out loud, "Amen." Then silently wait until your partner has also said "Amen" out loud. Squeeze each other's hands and know that you have taken a big step in the discipline of praying together.

3. Finish silent prayer out loud. The third way you can pray together is an extension of the second way we have just described. It takes us a step further in becoming more open and more comfortable praying together. Instead of ending your silent prayer with a verbal "Amen," agree that after a squeeze of the hand, one of you will finish the silent prayer out loud. Just say out loud something that acknowledges feelings of thanksgiving and praise for the knowledge that God is present with you and that he hears not only your prayers but the needs of your hearts. Or you may simply thank him for being present with you, both in your time of prayer and in your time of conversation. You may want to alternate who does the "out loud" praying each time, making cer-

.ch of you becomes more comfortable hearing your
as, in the presence of your spouse, you talk to God.

ut prayers, then share them. Another way a couple can
pray out loud together is for each person to first write
ort, simple prayer that is meaningful to him or her. Do
part separately. Then come together and read your prayers
out loud. After you finish, you may want to discuss what positive
responses you have to each other's prayer and how it felt for you
to talk out loud to God together.

5. Pray as you talk. In this step, we back up and include God
more consciously in our preliminary conversation together.
Twice a year Jan and I get together with four other couples for a
weekend. We are from different parts of California, so once a year
those up north plan the weekend, and the other time we down
south plan it. We've been doing this for over twelve years. One of
the highlights of the weekend is our time of conversation together about ourselves, our marriages, and our kids. Often, as we
talk together, someone will stop the conversation and suggest we
pray about what we've just been talking about. One or two pray,
then we move back into conversation.

As a couple, you can simply stop in the middle of the conversation and suggest "let's pray a moment." At first, you can pray silently, but then, as you become more comfortable, you can
simply add God to the conversation. For example, when Jan and I
are talking, one of us might simply say, "Lord, you are here listening as we talk, and we want to acknowledge your presence and
ask for your help with this situation." It may even be simpler
than that, or one of us may add another sentence or two; the person praying may or may not say "Amen," and then we go back to
our conversation. Over time, God's place within your conversations will become more natural, and you will become more aware
of his presence.

6. *Pray out loud, together, daily.* This step is something Jan and I have been doing as a couple for many years. I'm not certain when we began—I know it was not in the beginning of our marriage. But somewhere around the ten- or fifteen-year mark, we started praying together, out loud, every night as we went to bed. We pray about our needs, our parents, our kids, and their kids. We pray for each other, and we pray for specific situations that are going on in our life and in the lives of our friends and extended family.

Over the years, as we've become comfortable with praying this way, we have expanded our practice to other times of the day. One of us may feel the need to pray, so we stop and pray. It is more than a part of our conversation—we are purposely stopping to pray. Even when I travel, we talk on the phone in the evening. We always use that time to pray together as well.

It's interesting what happens at home when we have had a disagreement. Perhaps it's been a very relationally cool evening. One of us is angry at the other, or, more likely, we're both upset and angry. As we get into bed, one of us will finally say, "Are we going to pray?" I can recall times when my answer has been, "No, I don't feel like praying." Often in those situations, after a few minutes of silence, Jan will say something like "Well, I'm going to pray," and she begins. By the time she's finished, my own heart has softened enough to join her and pray as well. Of course, there are times when neither one of us will say anything except maybe "Lord, you know we're in trouble here," and then prayer together awaits the next day.

7. *Practice "vulnerable prayer."* This one is difficult, and Jan and I don't do this type of praying together very often. We're still working on it. In vulnerable prayer, we pray about ourselves, out loud, in the presence of our spouse. We are comfortable enough with each other that we can bring our weaknesses, our failures, our

struggles, and with a lot of vulnerability, talk openly with God in the presence of our partner.

Don't Put the Last Step First!

I think that often, when a wife tells her husband that she wants them to pray together, it is this vulnerable type of prayer that flashes through his mind and causes him to go silent. This type of prayer is listed as number 7, not because it is the "best" way to pray together, but because it is the most difficult way to pray together. It may take a couple fifteen years of praying out loud together before they even begin to approach this type of prayer. Other couples may never pray this way together, while some will find that this type of prayer makes their spiritual intimacy most meaningful. The important thing is to pray together. If you can pray vulnerably together, fine. If not, that's fine as well.

What Jan and I have found is that there are times when we can pray this way together, and then there are times when we simply don't even think to pray this way. Remember, the goal is simply to pray together—to acknowledge God's presence in our marriage. Find a way to begin, if you haven't already. And then keep on doing it. This is one of the important ways we can participate with God in what he is already doing all around us.

HOW PRAYER CAN MAKE YOUR MARRIAGE BETTER

We've all heard that "the couple that prays together stays together." It's true. Praying together does more than bring two people into the presence of God, as powerful as that is! It also knits two hearts together. It opens communication, forces us to slow down the hectic pace of our life so that we can talk before we pray, and it keeps us aware that it isn't just the two of us, struggling along. God is also a part of "the two of us."

TO TALK ABOUT TOGETHER

- Talk about some of the ways you have tried to pray together in the past. Which ones have been most easy or natural? Which ones have been more difficult?
- Four reasons were given in this chapter for why praying together is difficult. Which of the four best describes some of your own hesitations?
- What are some of the things each of you could do in order to overcome that difficulty?
- Describe the first step you can take to either begin praying together or to expand the ways you already pray together as a couple. Set a time to begin.

FIVE

Words of Life:
Nourishing Your Marriage

ON our radio program one day we were discussing spiritual intimacy in marriage. We had mentioned the discipline of study and meditation, and a woman called in; she said that the way she and her husband studied the Bible together did not help her develop any sense of spiritual intimacy with him. "In fact," she added, "all that happens is that every time we have a Bible study together, I end up seething with anger and resenting him."

I asked her to give me an example of what took place when they had Bible study together, and she described what I would refer to as a formal Bible study. Her husband was the teacher and she was the student—always! "Not only is he always the teacher," she exclaimed with emotion, "he isn't a very good teacher, for he's always got to be right. My opinions mean nothing to him. It usually ends up with him telling me what I'm supposed to be learning, and I sit there silently angry. I don't know how much longer I can be silent!"

I know very few couples who can handle doing a formal Bible study together. The teacher-student arrangement certainly isn't conducive to a growing sense of partnership! And partnership is what the spiritual disciplines within marriage are meant to build. Bible study done as a couple should not involve one person being in the position of authority. Both partners are learners, and the Holy Spirit is the teacher.

> *I know very few couples who can handle doing a formal Bible study together.*

TAKING THE MYSTERY OUT OF MEDITATION

What, exactly, is study and meditation? And what is its ultimate purpose in a marriage relationship? Study and meditation are tools for helping us focus on what God is doing around us and in us. Paul urges us, "Fix your thoughts on what is true and good and right. Think about things that are pure and lovely, and dwell on the fine, good things in others. Think about all you can praise God for and be glad about. . . . and the God of peace will be with you" (Phil. 4:8-9).

First of all, we meet God in his Word. But we also meet God as we study how others have experienced the Word of God in their lives. Other words that describe meditation include *listening, reflecting, rehearsing* (within my thoughts), and *ruminating*. The goal is to incorporate what we have understood—so that we experience change in our life as a result. These are not always big changes; sometimes they're not even visible to an outsider. But we aim to be in the process of transformation as a normal part of life.

I was talking with a couple recently who were having a very difficult time in their marriage. The husband wanted the marriage to not only work but to improve. The wife was very reluctant and even resistant to what we were trying to do in counseling together. In a session with her alone she acknowledged that she wasn't even certain she wanted to stay in the marriage.

They took a week's vacation together, and when they came in for their next session, everything was different. The wife said that one night, while visiting her sister, she had grabbed a book off her sister's bookshelf. When she couldn't sleep, she read some of the journals of John Wesley. She was deeply moved by how this man of God described his own sinfulness and unworthiness. She said, "How can I think I'm so great when this great man of God felt he was so sinful and worthless?"

For several days she meditated on her reactions to what she had read and then shared them with her husband. It marked a breakthrough in their relationship, not only because of what was going on inside of her spiritually and emotionally, but also because of some spiritual intimacy they were beginning to experience together as she shared with her husband what God was teaching her.

FOUR TIME-TESTED HANDLES
IN STUDY AND MEDITATION

1. Repetition. I remember reading an old book some years ago entitled *The Seven Laws of Teaching.* The first law was to "repeat, repeat, and repeat" what you want your students to learn. The author went on to suggest that each time through, the material needed to be presented differently from the previous time, but the law was simple—learning takes place through *repetition.* This author was also describing the first requisite to effective study and meditation.

Frankly, I get frustrated with repetition. I believe I can and should learn something the first time. I don't ever like to read something more than once. I have a friend who has read a classical historical novel at least six times. Once when he was beginning to read it again, I asked, "How can you read it again when you know what is going to happen?" And he said, "I just enjoy reading it because it's so well written. And besides, I discover something new every time I read it." Well, his point of view, not mine, reflects this first principle of study and meditation—the value of repetition.

How does this relate to what we do as a couple? Obviously there is value in repeating the study of something so that we can meditate more effectively on what we have read. For example, sometimes we want to read through a book of the Bible together and then move on to another book. Why not take a short book like Philippians and, over the course of a month or so, read it seven or eight times? Perhaps you read a chapter a day and then begin over again. Or you may read the first chapter once a day for a week and then move on to chapter two. Don't shy away from repetition. It's the foundation of this discipline.

2. Concentration. If we begin with repetition, concentration comes more easily. We're not just studying so that we can get a grade in some class, but so that we may experience more of God together, and that means we need to concentrate on what God is saying to us.

The Israelites were told to do certain things with God's commandments. In a way, this was to help them concentrate on what God was doing in their lives. Moses told the people to "keep these commandments carefully in mind. Tie them to your hand to remind you to obey them, and tie them to your forehead between your eyes! Teach them to your children. Talk about them when you are sitting at home, when you are out walking, at bedtime, and before breakfast!" (Deut. 11:18-19). That's concentration!

One way you can help your concentration is to make notes on

three-by-five cards that you carry around with you. At different parts of the day, look through the notes on your cards as a reminder of what God is doing in your study together and in your marriage. When some special insight strikes you, take the time to call your spouse and share your discovery with him or her.

3. Understanding. We want to understand what God is saying to us, for only when we have understanding can we make God's Word work within our lives. That's why it's so important to experience this discipline *with someone.*

I recently accepted a position where I am to direct a large psychological clinic that has a number of specialized clinics within it. As I was preparing for this responsibility, I read through the brochures, the stacks of files containing minutes of meetings, organizational charts, and lists of urgent issues that needed to be dealt with. My "study and meditation" on all of this material gave me some sense of "understanding" the various organizations I would be overseeing. But it was only when I could sit down with the individual directors and ask questions that I finally had any real understanding of what I had gotten myself into.

That's why it is so important that, when it comes to this discipline together, we not only study and meditate but also discuss what we are studying and meditating upon. Often, understanding can take place only when we are able to sit down with someone else and talk about what we are seeking to understand.

4. Application. Once we have understanding, we need to apply it to the life we're actually living. Sometimes the application is made obvious by the Holy Spirit. Jan and I are often amazed at how a particular passage of Scripture or a specific devotional or a section of a book that "just happens" to fall into our hands can speak so directly to a current situation in the life of one of us or in our shared life.

But sometimes the Spirit allows us to search for the application and struggle and work with it. Sometimes we do this simply by asking each other "What is God saying to us here?" and then taking the time to meditate—to focus—on what we have been studying.

✝ MAKING BIBLE STUDY AND MEDITATION
A VITAL PART OF LIFE TOGETHER
There are numerous ways for a couple to study and meditate together. Here are just a few.

Devotional books. This is an easy way to begin—the material is ready-made and doesn't put pressure on either one of you to come up with "spiritual" thoughts or creative prayers. I think the best way to do this would be to take turns reading the daily devotional to each other. You may find a better way that works for you. There are several good devotionals written specifically for couples, but a good general devotional can be just as valuable. Some denominations provide devotional materials. For example, liturgical churches, such as Catholic and Episcopal, have various devotional booklets that incorporate the Scripture passages that follow the lectionary for the church year.

Other books about the Book. Read a book together, and discuss what you are reading. In the appendix we list a number of books you could read and discuss together.

There are several ways to read a book together. Some couples will read the same book, but one person after the other. Each person has a different color of pen and marks passages that are particularly meaningful. Of course, the second person reading the book has the benefit of seeing what the first person marked. But when the second person has finished, the couple will set a time to sit down and leaf through the book, commenting on what they have marked. They talk together about what struck them as they read—what meaning it had in their lives, or why what struck the one person didn't even catch the attention of the other. I know some couples who are disciplined enough to do this one chapter at a time—each one reading it through and marking it, then sitting down and talking before moving on to the next chapter.

The Bible. Some couples want to begin with the Bible, for they believe the Word of God is primary. What my wife and I have found to be enjoyable is for one of us to read a passage of the Bible out loud to the other person. Usually I read to Jan. As I do, I will often stop reading because something strikes me, or just as often, Jan will stop me and comment on something that strikes her. Sometimes that comment will lead to a discussion, and sometimes we just go back to reading.

In one sense, this could be called a Bible study, but it would be an inductive approach to Bible study. This approach often has no formal teacher, but it begins with an attempt to understand what the text is saying, both within the context of the passage as well as what it is saying directly to me. Then we look at what we think the author meant when he wrote that passage. Finally we look at what that passage means in our life together. How do I apply it to me? How do we apply it to us? Inductive Bible study is a study done by partners who together seek to understand and apply the Word of God to their lives. Sometimes our shared Bible reading becomes that type of study.

A class. If you are not structured enough to begin with any of the first three suggestions, try taking a class together. Sign up for an elective class in your Sunday school. If you live near a Christian college or seminary, ask about taking a class together. Most colleges allow outsiders to audit classes, rather than going through a regular program. Think of it as your "marriage" taking the class, so that all of the work you do for that class is done together.

If you are in a Sunday school class or attend a church service together, take the Sunday school lesson or the sermon as an opportunity to exercise this discipline of study and meditation. Instead of critiquing the lesson or the sermon, take the time to reread the main passage of Scripture. Discuss that passage and seek to understand what it is saying to each of you, adding any insights you remember from the lesson or the sermon.

Nonverbal "books." Isaiah tells us that "the mountains and hills, the trees of the field—all the world around you—will rejoice. Where once were thorns, fir trees will grow; where briars grew, the myrtle trees will sprout up. This miracle will make the Lord's name very great and be an everlasting sign [of God's power and love]" (55:12-13). Remember that God is already at work all around you. That work is within people, but it is also seen in all of creation. Become a student of life—all forms of life. Develop an attitude that looks for God everywhere—in nature, in other people, even in your spouse and within yourself. Talk together about what you are discovering and observing. As the two of you develop this discipline of study and meditation, you will be drawn into a deeper shared intimacy with God our Creator.

How Study and Meditation Can Make Your Marriage Better

Marriages never stand still, even though they may feel that way at times. Either a husband and wife are growing closer together, or they are growing further apart. Either they are healthy and growing healthier, or they are sick and becoming more unhealthy. One of the best ways to keep your marriage growing in a healthy direction is to feed it, and the discipline of study and meditation gives you that food.

When the two of you are studying and meditating upon the same material, God has twice the opportunity to teach you! This kind of learning together also provides more opportunity for

---

*Marriages never stand still, even though they may
feel that way at times.*

---

accountability; it's not as easy to go against a scriptural principle
if both of you have been studying and discussing it. The simple
fact that you have talked with another person about what you are
studying means that you will remember much more of the material. Find a method and style of study and meditation that you
can work with as a couple. And give it time to reap some real
benefits in your marriage.

---

*It's not as easy to go against a scriptural principle if
both of you have been studying and discussing it.*

TO TALK ABOUT TOGETHER

- Talk about some of your efforts to study and meditate
  together. Which ones have been satisfying? Which ones
  have been frustrating? Discuss why.
- Think again about the four parts of study and meditation: repetition, concentration, understanding, and application. Is there a place in that process where you get
  bogged down when you try to study and meditate together? Talk about which of the four parts of study and
  meditation are most difficult for you.
- Decide which of the ways you are going to begin to
  study and meditate together, or if you are already doing
  this, discuss how you can expand or improve upon your
  present practice.

SIX

When Submission Applies to All:
Making a Way for Unity

ABOUT two-thirds of the way through my first session with Sue and Bart, I noticed that Bart was getting impatient. I asked him what he thought the major problem was, and, with a sigh of relief that he could finally say it, he pointed out, "Doc, we wouldn't have any problems if she'd just be a biblical wife."

I suspected that I knew what Bart meant, but I asked him to be more specific. "Well," he continued, "she just isn't submissive anymore. And wives are supposed to submit to their husbands, aren't they?" I paused for a moment and then answered, "Of course they are, but aren't husbands supposed to submit to their wives as well? How long has it been since you've submitted to her?" As he started to protest, I pointed him to Ephesians 5:21, which preceded his favorite passage. Paul urges each of us to "honor Christ by submitting to each other."

Bart's attitude is a good picture of what is probably the most common abuse of the spiritual discipline of submission. Submission is something only wives are supposed to do—husbands are only asked to "love their wives." It's amazing how sermons can be reconstructed and Scriptures ignored in order to perpetuate something that is so opposed to what Jesus lived and taught.

One of the reasons I believe that the Barts of our world have trouble with the idea of submission is that our culture emphasizes competition. Men are raised in an atmosphere of competing. It begins on the playground, moves to the baseball diamond, and then continues on as men struggle with who has the best job and makes the most money. Men who don't like to compete are often seen as somehow less masculine than those who thrive on competition.

In many ways, the discipline of submission will either make or break your efforts to develop spiritual intimacy together. Over the years I've talked with many couples, and probably the most common problem has been this area of submission. Sue and Bart are a typical representative of these couples.

What Does It Mean to "Submit"?

If competition is the antithesis of submission, what else might we say about this discipline? Submission is being able to give up my rights for the good of others. In the biblical sense, submission goes even further. Sometimes we can give up our rights on the outside, but inside we are clinging tightly to what "should have been" ours. Biblical submission focuses on the spirit within us as we give up our rights. If we truly relinquish our rights, that act takes place in our spirit, the very core of our being. What we say on the outside we mean on the inside. When we understand that spirit, we can also better understand Jesus' words when he said, "Love your *enemies!* Pray for those who - *persecute* you!" (Matt. 5:44).

Several years ago, one of the books I was writing was supposed to be included in a special series. I was excited about its inclusion. But as we approached the publication date, the publisher said that the people who controlled the series did not want my book included. Changes were made to the cover, and the book was released on its own. This was a real struggle for me. Didn't they like my book? Did they dislike me? Was there something wrong with the project? No one could give me an answer.

Finally, I decided to give up my right to know, or even to understand. I made that decision without any assurance that there was any good that could come out of it. Basically, I was letting go of something that hadn't gone my way. I knew, though, that letting go on the outside really didn't make any difference if I didn't have the same submission happening in my spirit. I decided that the best way I could know I was developing the right spirit was to pray for the success of the other people and for their series of publications.

At first I struggled. I wanted to compete. I thought about checking the sales figures to see if I had been "vindicated." But I didn't. Instead, I consciously followed through on my decision to pray. Recently I talked with one of the people involved in that earlier decision, and I felt a great freedom within. I genuinely wanted him to do well. And I was aware of his having the same desire for my success. Some of my questions were answered— others became unimportant. Our conversation was a wonderful example of the power of submission within an individual. There is even more power when it becomes a mutual part of a marriage relationship.

SUBMISSION REDEFINED BY THE LIFE OF JESUS

Why do we want to develop this discipline of submission? Is it simply another form of power? Sometimes it can be. We certainly can see the internal power that was in Jesus when he was submissive. For example, when he stood before Pilate, it's clear who was in control. When Pilate said that he had "the power to release [Jesus] or to crucify [him]," Jesus let Pilate know that "you would have no power at all over me unless it were given to you from above" (John 19:10-11). In other words, the only power Pilate had was what God allowed him to have. Jesus, who was in submission to the Father's plan, demonstrated strength and confidence in a frightening situation.

We see this discipline in every aspect of Jesus' life. Paul tells each of us—husbands and wives—that our "attitude should be the kind that was shown us by Jesus Christ, who, though he was God, did not demand and cling to his rights as God, but *laid aside his mighty power and glory,* taking the disguise of a slave and becoming like men. And he humbled himself even further, going so far as actually to die a criminal's death on a cross" (Phil. 2:5-8, italics added). This is the mind-set of true submission; we willingly lay aside our rights.

We see this in Jesus' behavior with the disciples, especially when they entered the upper room for their last supper together. As they approached this event, perhaps several of the disciples had been thinking back to the previous Sunday—now known as Palm Sunday—and were discussing who would play which role in the kingdom Jesus was certain to establish very soon. The concern was not only who would be the greatest (see Luke 9:46), but—and this was the unspoken concern—who would be the least.

As the disciples entered the room, there was a bowl of water and a towel on a table by the door. If there had been a host waiting for them, he would have washed each person's feet as they entered the room. Or if there had been a slave, that slave would have washed the guests' feet. When there was no host, each guest would wash someone else's feet and have his washed by another person. But not this evening. Not when visions of power and victory were floating in their minds. To wash one of the other disciple's feet might mean a lesser role in the coming government.

So everyone started to sit down, ignoring their dusty, dirty feet and the bowl of water and towel by the door. John tells us something of what Jesus was thinking. He writes, "how he loved his disciples!" (John 13:3). There was no attitude of disgust as his disciples made subtle plays for power; Jesus' heart was filled with love for these men. Then John says, "So he got up from the supper table, took off his robe, wrapped a towel around his loins, poured water into a basin, and began to wash the disciples' feet and to wipe them with the towel he had around him" (verses 4-5). Jesus, the one Peter had only recently said was "the Christ, the son of the living God," the one who had only a few days earlier ridden into Jerusalem to the cheers of the people, was now dressed like a slave as he washed his disciples' feet.

We can only imagine the guilt, remorse, and overwhelming regret each of the disciples felt. This wasn't what they had in mind! They didn't mean for Jesus to wash their feet. John writes, "When he came to Simon Peter, Peter said to him, 'Master, you shouldn't be washing our feet like this!'" (John 13:6). Peter expressed what each of the disciples must have felt.

When Jesus finished, he "sat down and asked, 'Do you understand what I was doing? You call me "Master" and "Lord," and you do well to say it, for it is true. And since I, the Lord and Teacher, have washed your feet, you ought to wash each other's feet. . . . You know these things—now do them! That is the path of blessing'" (verses 12-14, 17). An attitude of submission was, and still is, a path to blessing.

That evening, in the upper room, Peter learned a great lesson in genuine humility. The discipline of submission creates within us a true spirit of humility. Many years later, as he recalled the image of Jesus clothing himself with the towel as a slave, Peter wrote, "All of you, clothe yourselves with humility toward one another" (1 Peter 5:5, NIV).

So many times I have watched couples attempt to destroy each other in spite of their genuine love for each other. They are afraid to give up their right to be right. But sometimes they can recall that spirit of humility and live a life of loving submission to each other as an act of obedience to our Lord and Savior, Jesus Christ.

So many couples destroy each other because they are afraid to give up their right to be right.

THE CURSE REVISITED, THE CURSE REVERSED

Men will sometimes refer to Genesis 3:16 as the basis for a wife being submissive to her husband. The verse describes part of the woman's curse for sinning in the Garden: "Your desire will be for your husband, and he will rule over you" (NIV). If we look closely at this verse, we can see that it is written in a form of Hebrew poetry called parallelism, in which the same general point is made by two statements that are either similar or directly opposite each other. Read as parallelism, the verse could just as easily say, "Your husband will rule over you, and your desire will be to overthrow him." This certainly describes much of what I've seen take place in most husband/wife conflicts. There is a subtle, and sometimes not so subtle, competition for power, and it is part of our sinful, human condition as a result of the Fall.

We made the point back in chapter 1 that part of the purpose of Christian marriage is to reverse the curse on Adam and Eve. We want to restore to some degree what was lost back in the Garden. If that is true, then one of the purposes of Christian marriage is to reverse this pattern of the husband ruling over the wife and the wife seeking to overthrow his leadership. When we understand and seek to develop the discipline of submission in our marriage, leadership is shared. We are reversing the curse and finding in its place blessing and joy.

One of the goals of Christian marriage is to "reverse the curse" of the husband ruling over the wife and the wife seeking to overthrow his leadership.

 MAKING SUBMISSION A VITAL PART
OF LIFE TOGETHER

Learning a lifestyle of submission is not a matter of memorizing a few select verses (and quoting them regularly at one another!). We can allow the Scriptures to guide our minds and hearts as we take specific steps.

1. Figure out where you're competing. Since we have identified competition as the opposite of submission, take some time together and identify areas of your marriage in which you compete with each other. I know that in the early days of our marriage, I competed with Jan in the area of work. For several years, we both worked in a bank. Although we worked for the same bank, we worked in different offices. When she got a promotion, I was happy. But underneath I felt driven to work my way up somehow. I couldn't get promoted, so I talked instead about how quickly I did my work as a teller, and how accurate I was. A big part of this was a subtle form of competition with Jan.

I've seen couples who have competed with each other to be the better parent, not realizing that this enabled their child to wrap them around his or her little finger. Sometimes we compete in the area of friendship, or in social settings. Others even compete in athletics. I remember one wife who finally admitted to her husband that she had pretended to lose interest in tennis because of how he reacted every time she beat him. He would never have admitted to it, just as I would never have admitted to competing with Jan at the bank. But when it's all over and we look back, we can see the competitive spirit one or both of us experienced.

As you talk about ways you compete, talk also about how the discipline of submission would soften and eliminate the spirit of competition. Pray together about ways you could affirm and support each other in a spirit of love and humility.

2. Look at how, as a couple, you make decisions. Is it always one-sided? Have you compartmentalized your decision making? For example, in your marriage, does the wife make all the decisions about the kids and the home? Does the husband make all the decisions about job choices and locations, about money and investments?

By the time our youngest son reached adolescence, Jan and I had developed an unhealthy pattern. Since he was the "baby" in the family, Jan was very protective of him. If I started to "interfere" by trying to discipline him, he would react and Jan would step between us. Each of us knew that when it came to disciplining that son, I was out of the loop—Jan made the decisions.

When we both saw what we had created, we sat down and discussed our pattern of behavior. I remember suggesting that my son and I could work it out if she would just not jump in. Surprisingly, she agreed. Sometime later, my son and I started to get into it, and Jan stayed silent and left the room. When our son saw it was just him and me, we did begin to work it out, and over the next months we established a better pattern. One time I asked Jan why she had to leave the room, and she said it was the only way she could stay out of the "discussion" we were having. In that situation, she had to work on her discipline of submission.

Once you have identified areas of decision making within your marriage that are one-sided, talk about them. Not every decision must be made jointly. But make certain both of you are aware of which decisions do need to be made by both of you. Develop ways of making sure the two of you are involved in these particular situations.

Make certain both of you are aware of which decisions need to be made by both of you.

---

3. *Exchange roles.* This is a good way to break down existing patterns so that you can better understand them. This is especially helpful when you are at an impasse on what is really at stake in your discussion. In exchanging roles, you stop your discussion and agree to take the opposite position for perhaps five minutes. For example, if Jan and I had been unable to work out the lopsided way we were disciplining our son, we could have stopped, and then I would argue as if I were taking her position on the issue and she would argue as if she were taking my position on the issue. In other words, I attempt to "convince" her of what she already believes, and she attempts to "convince" me of what I already believe.

I've had couples resist doing this on their own, so I've asked them to switch roles and continue their argument in my office. I usually find that the resistance comes because one of them hasn't really been listening to the other person and cannot "argue" the opposite point of view. The spirit of the discipline of submission calls upon each of us to listen humbly to what our partner is saying. Often when we really are listening, the problem quickly resolves itself.

4. *Switch authority.* You can also exchange "leadership" and learn a lot about yourselves and the situation. One of the things I do

with couples who struggle with this is to suggest that on odd-numbered days the husband is in charge of everything in the home, and on even-numbered days the wife is in charge of everything. Or the husband is in charge on Monday, Wednesday, and Friday, and the wife is in charge on Tuesday, Thursday, and Saturday. They often wonder about Sunday, and I suggest they find some way to be fair about Sundays. Working out that little leadership problem often helps them work out other leadership issues.

5. *Learn how to compromise.* Before I became a counselor, my attitude toward any kind of compromise was that it was a sign of weakness. Obviously, you can see the root of some of Jan's and my problems during those years. We often tell couples at retreats that the first ten to twelve years of our marriage were very difficult, and then I wised up, got my priorities straight, and learned how to compromise.

There are two ways to look at a good compromise. The first is from the negative point of view. In a good compromise, neither party gets everything they want. They both have to give up some things that are important to them. The other way to look at a good compromise is from the positive point of view. Both parties get some of the things that are important to them. If one person is giving up what is important all of the time, then you are not compromising with each other.

What happens when one partner feels that God is calling them to do something that will have significant impact on them as a couple, but the other person does not have that same sense of God's calling? The discipline of submission recognizes that "if it is not God's will for both of us, then it is probably not God's will for one of us." When we are married, *God leads us as a couple.* Until we both sense God's leading we are either premature in our decision or we are mistaking God's call. Paul's advice in Ephesians 5:10 applies as we learn to compromise: "Learn as you go along what pleases the Lord." If he had been writing specifically to a married audience, Paul might have said, "Learn as you *go along together* what pleases the Lord." That's the spirit of the discipline of submission.

The discipline of submission teaches us that if it is not God's will for both of us, then it is probably not God's will for one of us.

How Submission Can Make Your Marriage Better

One of the most common things I see in couples who are struggling in their marriage is that they are caught in a power struggle. A husband and wife will sit there and say things that are hurtful to the other person and harmful to the marriage because they are struggling desperately to prove to their mate that they are the one who is right. Couples have rehashed events for years, each one trying to show the other that "I am right, and you are wrong!" I sometimes ask, "What difference does it make who's right if the marriage suffers or dies?" Learning how to "honor Christ by submitting to each other" (Eph. 5:21) creates an atmosphere that can only improve any marriage.

TO TALK ABOUT TOGETHER
- In what ways have you as a couple continued to act out the curse described in Genesis 3:16—competing with one another for leadership?
- What belief systems will each of you have to change if

you are going to begin the process of reclaiming as a couple what was lost in the Garden?

- Not every area of married life needs to have "joint management." Some areas work best if one person takes the lead on a regular basis. In which areas of your marriage are you comfortable giving up "joint management"? (Don't assume you both agree on this question—spend some time talking about it.)
- Which one of you feels like you are being submissive most of the time? Does the other person agree or disagree? Talk about any differences in perception you might have.

SEVEN

Meaningful Worship:
Practice Makes Progress

MANY times, couples find that their personalities and backgrounds make it difficult for them to worship together. George and Janet hit it wrong on both counts. George marches to the beat of a different drum. He is in business for himself after struggling for a number of years working in the corporate structure. He doesn't like restrictions placed on his time or his energy. When he worked for a large company, he was always struggling with being late for work. Now that he has his own business, he's in his shop an hour before he opens for business. As he was growing up, his family belonged to a very structured, liturgical church, where worship followed the same predictable format every week.

Janet loves structure. She struggled for months about giving up the job she had had for eighteen years, in order to help George in his business. She loves predictability, and working for George doesn't provide too much of that. Janet's parents never took her to church. She started attending in high school and met George at his parents' church. She loves the predictable worship. "I can tell what's going to happen next based on what has just happened," she said, adding, "and I love it. It's one point in my life that feels stable." George, on the other hand, wants to attend a more char- ismatic church that one of his workers attends. "It sounds great to me. Nothing is ever the same two weeks in a row, except we know we're going to sing and the preacher's going to preach. As for what happens beyond that, God only knows from week to week." After a moment, George adds, "I've had enough of the same old thing, Sunday after Sunday, but Janet loves it, so I guess we'll keep going to the same old church together."

Many couples find that their personalities
and backgrounds make it difficult for
them to worship together.

Our personalities and our past experiences have a lot to do with the type of worship we are drawn toward and comfortable with. The problem with both Janet and George is that they are deciding on worship styles based on what is comfortable for them—*what do I get out of it?* This is part of worship. But to limit our understanding of worship to what *I* get out of it is to miss the point. Worship is di- rected toward God. It is centered not on me, but on Jesus Christ. While it is true that I need to feel a part of it, the focus is not on me.

That's where the idea of discipline in worship comes into play. If worship is going to be something we do together as a couple, and if this means that we have to get beyond our own comfort zones, then it will take practice. And perhaps the best place to practice is with each other.

WHAT DOES IT MEAN TO WORSHIP, ANYWAY?

Our word *worship* comes out of the Old English word *weorthscipe.* This word meant that someone ascribed "worth" to the object of their "weorthscipe," or worship. In our context as Christians, worship is the act, or actions, whereby we ascribe great worth to God. This is especially clear in the passage in Revelation where the twenty-four elders say, "O Lord, you are worthy. . . ." It is seen again in Revelation 5, where John hears "the singing of millions of angels surrounding the throne and the Living Beings and the Elders: 'The Lamb is worthy' (loudly they sang it!) '—the Lamb who was slain. He is worthy to receive the power, and the riches, and the wisdom, and the strength, and the honor, and the glory, and the blessing'" (verses 11-12). In both of these examples, "worth" is being rendered, or offered, to God.

One writer defined worship by saying that "in worship we engage ourselves with, dwell upon, and express the greatness, beauty, and goodness of God through thought and the use of words, rituals, and symbols."[1] In worship we meet with God and God meets with us.

✠ MAKING WORSHIP A VITAL PART OF LIFE TOGETHER
Many of us have placed a great limitation on worship. When you think of worship, do you think of Sunday morning church? Most of us do. But the discipline of worship carries the experience far beyond corporate, Sabbath worship. And, as a couple, you can experience worship in a number of ways.

Corporate worship. If you cannot agree on where you are going to worship, call a truce; put a time limit on it, perhaps three months. Then talk about ways you can compromise during this time in regard to your style and place of worship. Here are some suggestions you might consider.

Regardless of which service you are going to attend, before going to worship, take some time to pray together, asking God to

1. Dallas Willard, *The Spirit of the Disciplines* (San Francisco: Harper, 1988), 177.

The discipline of worship carries the experience far beyond corporate, Sabbath worship.

meet you as a couple in a fresh, new way. Ask him to prepare your hearts for what *he* wants you to experience together. Then plan to arrive at the service five to ten minutes early. Spend some time reading over the Scripture passage that will be read in the service. If that isn't printed in your bulletin, read over two or three psalms that you have agreed upon before coming to the service.

Use this time to prepare your hearts for worshiping together. As you meditate on the passages of Scripture, shut out what is going on around you and focus as much as possible on the majesty, power, and glory of God. Perhaps you can hold hands as you do this, and then pray silently for each other as the worship service begins.

When you leave the service, avoid the tendency to talk about what you liked or didn't like about the service of worship. Instead, take a moment to listen to what God has been saying to your own heart as you've worshiped together. Then, when you are alone together and can talk about the service, talk about what God was saying to you during the worship time. Perhaps it was during the singing or during the preaching. Perhaps it was something the pastor prayed. Perhaps it was related to the way the sunlight came through one of the windows. Whatever it was, focus your conversation on God, not on the actual components of the worship service.

This will not be easy to do. You may want to talk together about how hard it is for you. But know that the results are worth the effort. You are developing together the discipline of worship, and the joy of worship will come.

When George and Janet did this, it took several weeks for them

---

*When you leave a worship service, avoid the
tendency to talk about what you liked or
didn't like about it.*

---

to get beyond their differences and begin to listen to God's response to each of them during worship. George was surprised the most, for as he shifted his attention from what had become stuffy and predictable to him to what God wanted to say to him in the worship, he was pleasantly surprised. Then an interesting thing happened. As George became more open to "the same old worship service," Janet became more open to some of George's concerns and even offered to visit the other church some Sunday.

Worship with just the two of you. Spend some time learning different ways to worship when just the two of you are together. Paul tells us to "talk with each other much about the Lord, quoting psalms and hymns and singing sacred songs, making music in your hearts to the Lord" (Eph. 5:19). To the Colossians, Paul said, "Remember what Christ taught, and let his words enrich your lives and make you wise; teach them to each other and sing them out in psalms and hymns and spiritual songs, singing to the Lord with thankful hearts" (Col. 3:16). Our daughter-in-law, Terri, loves to sing. She was singing with her class of young children in Vacation Bible School recently, and one little girl said to her, "I wish my mommy would sing with me like you do." That little girl learned something about worship through singing. We adults can learn this important connection as well.

I remember a pastor some years ago saying that we learn most of our theology through the hymns and songs we sing. He was echoing what Paul was saying to us in both of these passages. He was also underlining the importance of spiritual songs and hymns. More than forty psalms command us to sing praises to God. And how much easier it is for us today. We have tapes and CDs to help us sing. Some of the very special times Jan and I have had in worship have been in our car on a trip. As we listen to praise music we will often sing along. Sometimes we stop the tape and talk about the meaning of a particular phrase and its importance to something in our lives at that point of time.

If you're not comfortable lifting your hands while you sing in church, or if that's not the way people sing in your church, perhaps you can experience lifting your hands before the Lord as you sing in your home or in your car. Lifting your hands as you sing isn't more or less worshipful than not lifting your hands— it's just a new, fresh way for some of us to sing and worship. To many, it is a tangible way to say, "I'm open to you, Lord."

Combine worship with prayer, study, and meditation. One of the ways we can pray is to give a prayer of praise. This is worship as we focus on some aspect of God's character. Here are some suggestions to help you study the Scriptures together and then incorporate the material into your times of praise:

Look up the different roles of Christ in the Scripture. For example, he is a prophet, a priest, a redeemer, a healer, a king, a shepherd, etc. Find Scripture that illustrates each, and then add that to your worship time. Remember that the angels in Revelation 5 focused their worship of Jesus on his being the Lamb of God. Do the same with the other roles of Christ.

Look up the different names of God. For example, Zechariah 6:12 calls God "The Branch;" Isaiah 9:6 gives several names to God, including "Mighty God"; Psalm 7:11 calls God a "judge who is perfectly fair." Make your own list and then find songs that focus on that facet of God's character.

Share the Lord's Supper together. Perhaps you think this can only take place in church. But some of Jan's and my most meaningful times have been in other places. Often when we do a couples' retreat, we end with a time of communion. Our favorite way of serving communion on a retreat is to serve the elements to each couple and then have them go off somewhere together to talk about the bread and the cup and then to return to partake with other couples.

Our family has traditionally celebrated communion together on Christmas Eve. After a time of sharing with each other, I will read the Christmas story from the Bible and then read about Jesus and the disciples having communion together in the upper room. Together we remind ourselves of why Jesus came as a baby—so that he could die on the cross, arise from the grave, and ascend into heaven where he sits at the right hand of God, making intercession for us. It's a time of worship for us around the table of the Lord.

We know other couples who shared communion as part of their wedding ceremony. They include communion as a part of each anniversary celebration, reminding each other that Jesus is a part of their shared life together. I think sharing communion as a couple one or two times each year, in your own way, is an important part of the discipline of worship together.

Involve body, mind, spirit, and emotions. Richard Foster, in *Celebration of Discipline,* writes that worship "involves our whole being. The body, mind, spirit, and emotions should all be laid on the altar of worship. Often we forget that worship would include the body as well as the mind and the spirit."[2] We worship with our whole being when we sing together, but are there other ways we, as a couple, bring our bodies into our worship?

Habakkuk tells us that "the Lord is in his holy Temple; let all the earth be silent before him" (Hab. 2:20). Have you ever sat in silence and watched a sunset? Then you know of one way to worship God in silence. Perhaps you've sat in some crowded

2. Richard Foster, *The Celebration of Discipline* (San Francisco: Harper & Row, 1988), 169.

place together in silence. Remember the first truth in our process of developing spiritual intimacy—that God is already at work around us. Why not look for God's activity? What might God be up to? After the silence, talk about your impressions. Notice the distractions. Do they have any special meaning to you? Learn to listen to the inner voice of the Holy Spirit as you sit in silence.

We had an interesting experience in worship recently. Our pastor asked us to think of something we would like to thank God for—something current in our life, whether small or large. Then he explained that after singing the next song, we were all to applaud, and that our applause would be directed to God. He talked about how we applaud great plays in sports, great performances in theater, and inspiring, courageous actions by other people. "Applause," he added, "is to give praise to someone worthy of that praise."

After we sang the chorus, the whole congregation applauded God, something we hadn't done as a congregation before. We had applauded God for general things before, but not for some particular involvement he had had in our lives. As we finished, Jan and I sat down and looked at each other, both knowing how special that moment had been for each of us. Here are the words to the chorus we sang:

> *We applaud Your greatness,*
> *We applaud Your might,*
> *And we shout to God in triumph*
> *As we set ourselves to fight;*
> *Ev'ry demon trembles*
> *When they hear our voices raised,*
> *Joined with loud applause affirming*
> *You are worthy to be praised.*[3]

3. Words and music by Rodney Johnson, © 1995 Refreshing Music/BMI, Adm. by Integrity Music, Inc.

As I write out these words, I am reminded of a time in Hawaii when we sat and watched a magnificent sunset. As the sun sank beneath the horizon, someone nearby began to applaud. Soon, people all around us applauded. As we joined in that applause, our thoughts were directed to the God of creation, and we were applauding his majesty. That's a physical expression of our worship together.

Be sure to worship during difficult times. It can be difficult to worship as a couple when our lives seem to be falling apart. During these seasons it becomes clear that worship is a discipline and that we must work together to praise God when it seems that there is nothing for which to praise him. Jan and I have found that these are the times when worship and praise have to become an absolute priority; otherwise, an excellent opportunity for spiritual intimacy will be lost.

Cultivating, as a couple, a holy dependency on God is part of the discipline of worship. During one very difficult time in our family, I remember trying so hard to help God with the needed miracle. I tried to arrange circumstances, but to no avail. Jan and I were out of sync with each other as well. Finally, I let go of my efforts, and together we were able to bind our hearts in that holy dependency on God to do or not do whatever he chose at that time. It wasn't easy, but it was a time of great growth together spiritually. And when God did act, it was beyond anything we could have imagined or controlled. *But it was the ability to worship God in the absence of any significant action by God that allowed us to depend upon his sufficiency.*

Cultivating, as a couple, a holy dependency on God is part of the discipline of worship.

How Worship Can Make
Your Marriage Better

For some of us, the thought of worship as a discipline is a contradiction. Worship is to be spontaneous. After all, some of the great worship experiences in the Bible occurred spontaneously. Look at Isaiah. He was simply going to the temple one day, perhaps grieving over the death of his king. And then, suddenly, he said,

> *I saw the Lord! He was sitting on a lofty throne, and the Temple was filled with his glory. Hovering about him were mighty, six-winged angels of fire. With two of their wings they covered their faces, with two others they covered their feet, and with two they flew. In a great antiphonal chorus they sang, "Holy, holy, holy is the Lord Almighty; the whole earth is filled with his glory." Such singing it was! It shook the Temple to its foundations, and suddenly the entire sanctuary was filled with smoke.*
> Isaiah 6:1-4

How could a person plan such an incredible event?

Or how can a "discipline" create the experience the apostle John describes for us in Revelation 4? He finishes his description by telling us that

> *when the Living Beings gave glory and honor and thanks to the one sitting on the throne, who lives forever and ever, the twenty-four Elders fell down before him and worshiped him, the Eternal Living One, and cast their crowns before the throne, singing, "O Lord, you are worthy to receive the glory and the honor and the power, for you have created all things. They were created and called into being by your act of will."*
> Revelation 4:9-11

Our Eyes Are Opened

Both these events appear to be quite spontaneous, but we should keep in mind the two people who witnessed them. One was a man who had demonstrated such a spirit before God that God commissioned him to be a prophet. The other was Jesus' beloved apostle, so seasoned a disciple and such a threat to a hostile government that he had been exiled to an island. The eyes of these believers beheld marvelous scenes of worship—because they had already learned to see God, to be aware of God's work, and to know how to respond to their Lord. No doubt any number of people could have been in the temple with Isaiah that day—yet he was the one who saw the Lord. John was probably not the only person on that island—yet Revelation was given to *him*. Worship is more a matter of our spirit than of the place we're in or even the people we're with.

We Discover God's Presence

When we describe worship as a discipline, we are talking about what Brother Lawrence, a seventeenth-century monk, described; we are "practicing the presence of God" in our lives on a regular basis. Brother Lawrence wrote, "I cannot imagine how religious persons can live satisfied without the practice of the presence of God."[4]

Brother Lawrence was a humble monk whose life was very routine and boring. He worked in the monastery kitchen most of his life. If one were to look at the externals of his life, he would hardly attract any attention. But as he went about the mundane events of his daily existence, he developed the discipline of constantly being aware that God was present with him. As he peeled potatoes, he practiced an awareness of God's presence. As he swept the kitchen floor, God was there with him.

4. Brother Lawrence, *The Practice of the Presence of God* (Nashville: Upper Room, 1950), 32.

When he went to worship, it was easy for him to know that God was there also, for he had experienced God's presence with him in the kitchen.

It also worked wonders with his own attitude toward his kitchen duties. If my inner focus is on God's presence with me as I scrub the pots and pans, who notices the grimy dishwater? Brother Lawrence added, "The time of business does not with me differ from the time of prayer; and in the noise and clatter of my kitchen, while several persons are at the same time calling for different things, I possess God in as great tranquility as if I were upon my knees. . . ."[5] This kind of attitude doesn't just happen; it's a way of thinking only arrived at through discipline.

There is also a sense of freedom we experience as a result of the discipline of worship. The soul of the worshiper knows the truth of the chorus, "Set my spirit free, that I may worship thee." There is also a spirit of humility as well as a contentment that comes from this kind of worship. And, as Brother Lawrence demonstrates, out of this freedom within our worship comes our ability for genuine service.

If you and your partner could develop the discipline of worship, how might it affect your life together? You can become more closely bonded as you participate in mutual worship. When all of your tasks—household chores, issues with the children, concerns about aging parents, paying the bills—become, in your minds, acts of worship, the days and even dark seasons become filled with more meaning and purpose. And when all of life becomes part of our ongoing worship, all of life can strengthen the marital relationship. Paul's words to the Colossians also apply to our marriages: "And whatever you do or say [as a couple], let it be as a representative of the Lord Jesus, and come with him into the presence of God the Father to give him your thanks" (Col. 3:17).

5. Ibid., 26.

TO TALK ABOUT TOGETHER

- Discuss what type of worship is most meaningful to each of you. Describe times when you have experienced that type of worship.
- In what ways have you limited your experience of worship together? How can you become more open, together, to other ways to worship?
- Which of the six ways to worship together as a couple looks like a good starting point for you? Be specific as to when and where you will begin, or what you will add to, the discipline of worship in your marriage.

EIGHT

Celebration:
The Habit of Enjoying Life

LET'S celebrate!"

How often have we said that after receiving some wonderful news? But what does it really mean to celebrate? We've all worked at having a "good time" to the point of exhaustion. We've all had fun, even while feeling empty inside. There must be more to real celebration than "having a good time."

WHAT IS THERE TO CELEBRATE?

Dallas Willard says that celebration "is the completion of worship, for it dwells on the greatness of God as shown in his goodness *to us*" (italics his).[1] In worship, our focus is on God and his characteristics. *In celebration, we focus on what God is doing around us and in our lives.* Celebration is what we do when we enjoy ourselves, our life, and our world *in conjunction with* our faith and trust in Jesus Christ.

1. Dallas Willard, *The Spirit of the Disciplines* (San Francisco: Harper, 1988), 179.

---

*Celebration is what we do when we enjoy ourselves,
our life, and our world, in conjunction with
our faith and trust in Jesus Christ.*

The King's Party

As King Solomon begins his writings in Ecclesiastes, his attitude toward life seems pretty cynical. He writes, "In my opinion, nothing is worthwhile; everything is futile. For what does a man get for all his hard work?" (Eccles. 1:2-3). This type of cynicism leads many of us to say, "So strike up the band, break out the booze, and let the party begin!" Since life is so horrible, we may as well party while we can.

Solomon doesn't start with the partying attitude, but he arrives there soon enough. First he seeks out wisdom only to conclude, "So I worked hard to be wise instead of foolish—but now I realize that even this was like chasing the wind. For the more my wisdom, the more my grief; to increase knowledge only increases distress" (1:17-18).

Then came the partying. He said to himself, "'Come now, be merry; enjoy yourself to the full.' But I found that this, too, was futile. . . . So after a lot of thinking, I decided to try the road of drink. . . . And then there were my many beautiful concubines" (2:1-3, 8). Again, he said that his search for pleasure ended up meaningless.

Solomon tried work, he tried achievement, he tried pleasure, and he tried wealth—all with the same conclusion: meaningless! Finally he arrived at this important insight about celebration: "Well, one thing, at least, is good: It is for a man to eat well, drink a good glass of wine, accept his position in life, and enjoy his work whatever his job may be, for however long the Lord may let him live. . . . To enjoy your work and to accept your lot in life—

that is indeed a gift from God" (5:18, 20). That's celebration!
Why? *Because this person has learned to accept life as a gift from
God.* The events of his daily experience are grounded in his
relationship with God.

Parties Planned by God

The Bible, especially the Old Testament, is filled with celebrations. One of the most interesting celebrations—which appears
to have never been practiced—was the Year of Jubilee. It is described in Leviticus:

> *Every fiftieth year, on the Day of Atonement, let the trumpets
> blow loud and long throughout the land. For the fiftieth year
> shall be holy, a time to proclaim liberty throughout the land to
> all enslaved debtors, and a time for the canceling of all public
> and private debts. It shall be a year when all the family estates
> sold to others shall be returned to the original owners or their
> heirs. What a happy year it will be!* 25:8-11

If Israel had followed this celebration, would there have been no
lasting poverty among its people? We can only speculate. Unfortunately, this is one celebration they ignored, even though they
had all the instructions for it. Apparently they didn't have the discipline for this kind of life-changing celebration.

Another celebration was related to the tithe. In Deuteronomy
14, Moses tells the people, "you must tithe all of your crops every
year. Bring this tithe to eat before the Lord your God at the place
he shall choose as his sanctuary" (14:22-23). This is nothing new
to our ears. But notice what comes next. Moses says, "If the place
the Lord chooses for his sanctuary is so far away that it isn't
convenient to carry your tithes to that place, then you may sell
the tithe portion of your crops and herds and take the money to
the Lord's sanctuary. When you arrive, use the money to buy an

ox, a sheep, some wine, or beer, to feast there before the Lord your God, and to rejoice with your household" (14:24-26). One translation includes in the instruction to buy "anything you wish" (NIV).

The tithe was for a celebration. It was to be used for a feast or to be sold in order to have a feast, but it was a feast that was shared with the Lord. That's what made it a celebration. Something changes when God is present in our celebration. For one thing, the emptiness is gone.

A Celebration That's Timeless: The Feast

The Jewish calendar is marked by a series of feasts, or celebrations. Each one is based on some historical event and marks some important way that God is involved with his people. There is the Feast of Tabernacles, or Booths, which commemorates the way God took care of Israel in the wilderness. There is the Feast of Weeks, which celebrates God's provision for his people at harvest time.

Each Jewish celebration is based on some historical event and marks an important way that God is involved with his people.

The single most widely practiced rite of Judaism in our country is a supper. It is the Passover seder. Here the mystery of God's participation changes a simple meal into a rich event filled with deeper meanings. Recently Jan and I watched a special PBS television program of one family's Passover seder. As the meal was consumed with a ceremony that retells an event thousands of years old, the symbols and the words drew us not only into that family's celebration, but also into the deeper shared experience related to that momentous past.

In the same way, when we come to the Lord's Table to share

the bread and the cup, the story of our Savior's death and resurrection is retold, and through the words and the event we are taken from the here and now into the most meaningful event in history. Our celebration, one that looks forward to our Savior's return, is a shared event with God himself. We are in the here and now, but in another way, we are also in the then and there. Celebrations can do that!

Other memorable celebrations in the Old Testament include the time Miriam "took a tambourine and led the women in dances. And Miriam sang" (Exod. 15:20-21). And her song was in praise of God. David, as he led the ark back into Jerusalem, "danced before the Lord with all his might and was wearing priests' clothing. So Israel brought home the Ark of the Lord with much shouting and blowing of trumpets" (2 Sam. 6:14-15). In each of these, there is excitement and joy, and God is central to the spirit of celebration.

One of the most profound celebrations in the New Testament is the party that the father gave the returning prodigal. When the older brother "returned home, he heard dance music coming from the house" (Luke 15:25) and asked what was going on. When he refused to join the party, his father said to him, "Look, dear son, . . . you and I are very close, and everything I have is yours. But it is right to celebrate. For he is your brother; and he was dead and has come back to life! He was lost and is found!" (verses 31-32). The older brother needed to come and enjoy the party!

HOW WE GOT TO BE SPIRITUAL STICKS-IN-THE-MUD

We've already noted that celebration needs to be a discipline because it is not something we will do on our own. What makes it so difficult? We are well rehearsed in standard excuses—too busy, too serious, life is too heavy, we're just not good planners. But excuses aren't our only hindrance to celebration.

Have you ever noticed how easy it is for a child to celebrate? When my granddaughter hears some pretty music on the stereo, she doesn't even stop to think about it—she starts to dance. She may dance for a moment and then go back to what she was doing. And then she may go back to dancing again. Her only problem with a celebration is that she hates for it to end and finds all kinds of ways to keep it going. Something happens to us between those joyful, celebratory childhood days and the days of our adulthood.

Sometimes, something does happen to us, literally. A parent leaves or dies; someone violates our personal boundaries and abuses us physically or sexually; a parent becomes seriously ill; a friend is killed. Any number of tragedies can strike, and the innocence of childhood vanishes.

And sometimes we spiritualize our childlikeness away, through faulty interpretations of Scripture, such as Paul's words in 1 Corinthians 13: "When I was a child I spoke and thought and reasoned as a child does. But when I became a man my thoughts grew far beyond those of my childhood, and now I have put away the childish things" (verse 11). But Paul is talking here about immaturity. It could just as easily be translated, "I have put away the immature things." Paul uses the word *childish,* not *childlike. Childish* means that we have refused to grow naturally into maturity—in our judgment, in our dealings with others, and in our life skills.

This is not the same as *childlike.* Jesus said, "Let the children come to me, for the Kingdom of God belongs to such as they. Don't send them away! I tell you as seriously as I know how that anyone who refuses to come to God as a little child will never be allowed into his Kingdom" (Mark 10:14-15).

Our need as adults to learn how to be *childlike* was highlighted for me recently when I spoke at the National Association of Christian Recovery annual convention. As part of their program, they provide a "play room" for the adults attending to have the opportunity to experience again what it is like to be childlike. Many people who are in recovery have lost a large part of childhood and never really had the chance to play or celebrate while they were growing up. At this convention, they have that opportunity, and many have found it to be an important part of their recovery and healing.

If you have difficulty celebrating with your spouse, take some time and reflect back on how you played as a child. Recall attitudes of the significant adults in your life during that time that either affirmed or belittled your play. Talk about these memories and then choose to experience the discipline of celebration in order to learn how to play together as a couple.

✝ MAKING CELEBRATION A VITAL PART
OF LIFE TOGETHER

Rethink your holidays. What do you do to make Easter, Christmas, Thanksgiving, birthdays, and anniversaries real celebrations? What do you remember your own family doing when you were a child? What traditions have you kept? As you look at your celebrations of these events and holidays, ask yourselves how, and if, your faith and God were included in the celebration.

Then take each one of these holidays and add what is needed in order to make it a real spiritual celebration. Remember that our first truth about spirituality is that God is already at work around us. That means he already wants to involve himself in our celebrations; all we need to do is slow down enough to recognize his presence.

Looking back, Jan and I wish we could have slowed down at Christmas. We felt this on Christmas Eve as we worked frantically into the wee hours of the morning, wrapping gifts and putting toys together for Christmas morning. Now that our children are grown, we do take time, both as a family and as a couple, to reflect on the true meaning of Christmas. But I wish we had slowed down years ago to better develop the discipline of celebration together.

If one of you has difficulty celebrating certain holidays, take the time to talk and pray together for healing. Perhaps that particular holiday was a painful part of your childhood. God wants to bring back the childlike part of you.

Look at your yearly calendar and see where the "holiday" gaps are. As our sons have married and grandchildren have arrived, our year is evenly spread out with celebrations. Make the most of each event. Come together to eat, to sing, to play, and to relate stories of God's actions in your lives. Then create some additional "holidays" to fill the gaps so that you have something to celebrate each month of the year.

Create some additional holidays to fill the gaps
so that you have something to celebrate
every month of the year.

Take some lessons from your kids. If you have trouble identifying what it is like to be childlike, let your children teach you. If you don't have children, allow the children of your friends to teach you about childlikeness. One way you can do this is to allow the children to help plan your celebrations. Pay close attention to the suggestions they give that you are inclined to ignore or dismiss. Talk with your spouse later about the meaning of those suggestions for you, and again, pray together for God's healing and/or wisdom in that place in your life.

Something to remember is that the child who is free to be a

child has no worries about tomorrow. He or she can fully enjoy the here and now. As adults, we need to recapture that freedom. This is the spirit of joy we want to infuse into our celebrations as adults. Laughter is rich and spontaneous in a child. Many of us need to learn to laugh again.

Do something you've been too busy to do. Is there a place you want to visit? A restaurant you want to try? Do it! Get your calendars out and write it in both of them—in ink. And then make certain it happens. What happens to Jan and me when we lose our ability to play is that we focus more intently on work and other pressures. In those times, all we know how to do is work. So we work at work and we work at home. We even work at playing. If this describes you, it will not be easy for you to stop working, but you must. If you don't, you'll miss the celebration!

Take the time to reminisce. When you are alone together at dinner, sit and talk. Relate stories to each other of God's activities in your life. Talk about how God brought you together as a couple. (He did, you know!) Talk about the fun times, and laugh while you talk. Talk also about the tough times and the lessons you learned from God.

Do the same when you are together with special friends. Talk about where you've been together as couples. The discipline of celebration shouldn't be a "heavy" time spiritually, although that may be a part of it at times. But underneath our conversation is a sense of joy, knowing that God has been a part of our journey together even when we were not aware of his presence.

C. S. Lewis reminds us of the everyday joys that can be a part of our discipline of celebration. In his book *The Screwtape Letters,* Screwtape (who is one of the lead devils and in charge of the apprentice, Wormwood) admonishes Wormwood for allowing his "patient" (who is one of us) the time to enjoy reading a book and to take a walk in the countryside. Celebration is the enjoyment of life, knowing that God is at work all around us. Screwtape, and all the devil's helpers, want to rob us of this joy. But the discipline of celebration helps us keep joy at the center of our lives together.

HOW CELEBRATION CAN MAKE YOUR MARRIAGE BETTER

For a long time, I resisted celebrations. Jan would set up special meals with the family and ask me to do something, and I would drag my feet. Later, when I saw how hurt she was, I would feel horrible. But the next celebration would come around, and I would drag my feet again. My resistance to celebrations was driving a wedge between Jan and myself.

It was only when I came to see celebration as a spiritual discipline that I was able to truly join the process. As Jan and I talked about the spiritual significance of a given celebration, both in terms of our marriage and of our family as a whole, I was finally able to connect the idea of celebrating with spiritual health and growth.

When we follow God's design,
our obedience is rewarded with joy.

When we follow God's design, our obedience is rewarded with joy. The old hymn said that there was "no other way to be happy in Jesus, but to trust and obey." This joyful spirit is promised by Jesus. One time, "as he was speaking, a woman in the crowd called out, 'God bless your mother—the womb from which you came, and the breasts that gave you suck!' He replied, 'Yes, but even more blessed are all who hear the Word of God and put it into practice'" (Luke 11:27-28). Blessed are those who are obedient in disciplines of the spirit.

Later, Jesus said the same thing even more clearly to his disciples: "When you obey me you are living in my love, just as I obey my Father and live in his love. I have told you this so that you will be filled with my joy. Yes, your cup of joy will overflow!" (John 15:10-11). Have you ever noticed that sense of joy within whenever you are doing what is right? That's what Jesus was talking about. As we establish habits of celebration, we add to our own joy, because we are being obedient to God.

When we make celebration part of our lifestyle, we are affirming that there is reason to celebrate. We announce, through our celebration, that we are citizens of heaven, that we live according to God's reality rather than the cynicism of this present world. The result is that when we can celebrate like this, "our deprivations and sorrows seem small, and we find in it a great strength to do the will of our God because his goodness becomes so real to us."[2]

This is why Paul can write to us and the Philippians from an Ephesian prison and repeat over and over that we are to rejoice. He is saying we are to rejoice regardless of our circumstances. Near the end of the letter he writes, "Always be full of joy in the Lord; I say it again, rejoice!" (Phil. 4:4). He knew that the joy that results from obedience will always be the antidote to despair.

When we can experience this kind of celebration in our marriage, circumstances cannot rob us of our joy.

Through celebration we announce that we live according to God's reality rather than the cynicism of this present world.

---

2. Ibid., 181.

EXPERIENCING GOD TOGETHER

TO TALK ABOUT TOGETHER

- In what ways do you as a couple celebrate the events of life? What special things do you always celebrate? What things do you wish you could celebrate more together?
- Talk together about the things that are fun for each of you. Discuss the areas of your lives in which one or both of you feel tied down and unable to celebrate. What might be standing in the way of your freedom to celebrate? Is there specific help you need to seek in order to be healed in that area?
- When is it difficult for you to be childlike? What event, or events, do you think make it difficult for you? In what ways will you be accountable to each other so that you can rediscover the celebration that comes so naturally to children?

NINE

Service That Serves Best:
Beyond Needs and Expecations

NEITHER John nor Sadie was excited when they were first asked to help out with the high school group. They were in their early thirties and hadn't even considered working with high schoolers, nor were they certain they would understand, or even like, this age group. But they agreed to consider this request and pray about their answer before coming to a final decision. As they talked and prayed together, both of them felt this was something God wanted them to do, so they agreed to offer themselves for service.

They have been serving now for over a year as resource people to the high school group at the church, and they are both more excited today than they thought they could be when they started. John said, "We're doing things we never even imagined doing. Last week Sadie spent the weekend away on a retreat with her small group of girls. They love her! I think it's been good for Sadie, for in many ways, it seems like she has become more alive since we started working with the high school group." Sadie added, "I feel more alive! I've really learned more about depending on the Lord in areas where before I felt totally inadequate. It has been fun, but most of all, it's drawn John and me closer together and closer to the Lord."

Their youth pastor loves what they are doing. To him, it is clear that both John and Sadie have a servant's heart. They didn't take on this responsibility because they were seeking the spotlight. In fact, there is little "glory" in the task. They just love being a part of the high school ministry. When I talked with the youth pastor, he said, "I wish I had more couples like John and Sadie. Nothing is too small for them to do. It's wonderful having them, for there are so many little things they do without even being asked."

There are all kinds of service opportunities around us, but not every act of service comes out of the spiritual discipline of service. Sometimes we serve simply out of love and compassion— our service is the result of our emotional response to a need we see (or sometimes our own need to help or to be needed). What kind of service comes out of spiritual discipline? We've discovered three distinguishing features.

Not every act of service comes out of the
spiritual discipline of service.

First, the discipline of service enhances my ability to follow Jesus more closely. Acts of service done out of a spirit of love and compassion may or may not do anything in terms of my own spirituality. They can simply be caring acts. But when service is a discipline, then my own spiritual life will by challenged by what I do.

Second, it is a service I would not be able to do apart from the Holy Spirit's work in my life. For example, Jesus says we are to love our enemies. Love is not my natural response. And sometimes loving my enemies means that I serve them in some way. That spirit of serving will be there only through the grace of God.

Third, we are exercising the discipline of service when we have a servant mind-set, which involves both motivation and a conscious decision to serve. As we will see a little later, there are several important ways that our servant mentality will affect our acts of service.

Jan and I struggle with this discipline, mainly because we get paid for things we do in this area. We have tried to develop the spirit of a servant and also stretch ourselves in what we do so that we are aware of a special dependence on God. Each time we go out to speak to couples, we remind each other of the privilege of the task and how dependent we are on God for his empowering.

Sadie and John demonstrated all three aspects of the discipline of service. They chose to serve in order to be obedient to Christ, and they are growing spiritually, both individually and as a couple, through their service. They are stretching themselves so that they are dependent on God to help them do the tasks. And they have the right spirit about it; they are servant minded.

Service That Leads, Leaders Who Serve

Jesus made it very clear on several occasions that leadership in his kingdom is based on servanthood. At one point the mother of James and John asked Jesus if her two sons could have thrones next to his. Jesus used that occasion to teach her, as well as the disciples, about servant leadership. He said, "Among the heathen, kings are tyrants and each minor official lords it over those beneath him. But among you it is quite different. Anyone wanting to be a leader among you must be your servant. And if you want to be right at the top, you must serve like a slave. Your attitude must be like my own, for I, the Messiah, did not come to be served, but to serve, and to give my life as a ransom for many"

(Matt. 20:25-28). We are to serve with a submissive spirit. We are to have a servant's heart.

We don't know much about the biblical couple, Priscilla and Aquila, but the little we do know confirms that they were servant leaders. We first meet them in Acts 18, where they meet Paul in Corinth after they have been exiled from Rome. While in Corinth with Paul, they help him in his ministry. Later, when Paul is forced to leave Corinth, Priscilla and Aquila leave with him. Sometime later in Ephesus, Priscilla and Aquila meet Apollos, a great preacher even though he knows very little about Jesus. Apollos only knows what John the Baptist had said about Jesus. At one point, after Priscilla and Aquila hear Apollos preach a "powerful sermon . . . they met with him and explained what had happened to Jesus since the time of John, and all that it meant!" (Acts 18:25-26). They didn't do this because they wanted their story to be included in the book of Acts! It appears that they had developed the discipline of service in their life together.

Nothing further is written about this servant couple until Paul ends his letter to the Romans. He sends greetings to Priscilla and Aquila, who have apparently returned to Rome, and then gives us another glimpse into their life of service. He says, "They have been my fellow workers in the affairs of Christ Jesus. In fact, they risked their lives for me, and I am not the only one who is thankful to them; so are all the Gentile churches" (Rom. 16:3-4). Paul also refers to this couple in his letter to the Corinthians, saying that they send their greetings. He gives us another glimpse into their service together by mentioning that a church met regularly in their home.

What a wonderful example of a husband/wife team who understood the discipline of service. Their effectiveness together speaks volumes about the quality of their spiritual intimacy with each other. One is never mentioned in Scripture without the other.

Serving with Power—and without It

We have described the discipline of service as being characterized by an attitude of serving. The picture becomes even more distinct when we compare the discipline of service with its opposite, which might be called self-centered service.

Self-Centered Service	The Discipline of Service
1. Comes through human effort	1. Holy Spirit enables
2. Wants the "big" event only	2. No act of service too small
3. Seeks external rewards	3. Content with <u>hiddenness</u>
4. Wants to pick and choose	4. Servant to all
5. Wants results	5. Wants relationship with God
6. Serves only when "wants to"	6. Serves out of choice[1]

We can't talk about the discipline of service these days without addressing the issue of codependency. For some time now, the wave of information about codependency has threatened to confuse our understanding of what it means to serve others. Some people want to avoid any appearance of codependency, and as a result, their service becomes more and more self-centered. Sometimes they become so self-absorbed that they end up neglecting to serve in any capacity.

Other people have reacted against teachings about codependency by rejecting the concept altogether. They just keep on serving and keep on taking responsibility for everyone in their lives. But as these people seek to help others, they are unaware that most of their motivation comes out of some internal need of their own: I will serve you because I need to meet my own needs. In this kind of situation a person is not really choosing to serve as much as he or she is following an impulse. Such a person will end up doing for others what the other persons can do for themselves. In the spiritual discipline of service, we do for others what

1. Based on ideas described by Richard Foster in *The Celebration of Discipline* (San Francisco: Harper & Row, 1988), 128–130.

they cannot do, or we help them do what they are too weak to do on their own at the present time.

Sometimes we get so involved in other people's lives that we have forgotten (or have never learned in the first place) how to nurture our own life and marriage. When this happens, we need healing before we can go on to serve. And sometimes healing requires that we withdraw, for a time, from serving others.

Debra's husband was thrilled when I told her to cut off all the things she was doing for everyone else. He didn't realize at the time that he was one of the "everyone else." There were a number of things Debra did for her husband that both of them simply took for granted. Now she changed directions. For example, she stopped acting as her husband's go-between with a number of people, including the children. If others had a problem with her husband, she decided they could discuss it with him. If he was gruff with one of the children, she stopped making excuses for him and told the child that he or she needed to talk with Dad about what he had done. She offered to go with them as they talked with Dad, but she stopped trying to explain his behavior to them. Debra resigned from her roles as a Sunday school teacher, as a Cub Scout leader, and as a classroom assistant. Very few people were happy with her decisions, for over the years, Debra had become a valued volunteer—you could always depend on her for what was needed!

As Debra spent almost a year in her self-imposed "retirement," she also looked at the influences in her life that had made it so important for her to take care of everyone else, at the same time neglecting her own needs and even the needs of her marriage. At the end of that year, Debra told me she had said yes to her pastor's request that she serve on the Christian Education Board. As I raised my eyebrows and prepared to ask her why, she added quickly, "but this is something I really want to do. And besides, I've said no to at least three other requests in the past two weeks." She had ceased to serve out of a drive to meet some unidentified needs of her own, and she was now beginning the discipline of service, in which her decisions were based on a different set of criteria.

She had ceased to serve out of a drive to meet needs of her own; now her service decisions were based on a different set of criteria.

Debra's withdrawal lasted for almost a year. I've known others who have only taken several months. *But some people never really understand the difference between codependent service and the discipline of service, and they never end their withdrawal.* The discipline of serving others is an important part of our relationship with God and an important part of our marriage relationship. But we need to clearly differentiate between the Spirit-guided-and -empowered discipline of service and service that begins and ends with the self.

Another concern that fades in importance when we exercise the discipline of service is the fear of being taken advantage of by the people we're serving. Jan resolved this issue some years ago when she decided to give money to some of the homeless people she encountered. Someone in our Bible study said to her, "How can you do that, knowing that they may just go and spend the money on drugs or alcohol?" After some discussion, our Bible study group agreed that we can give the money as if we are giving it to the Lord, without any concern for evaluating the possible use of the money. They felt it fit with Jesus' words: "When you did it to these my brothers you were doing it to me!" (Matt. 25:40). When our service is from a spirit of humility that is content with no one but God knowing what we are doing, no one can really take advantage of us.

> *When we are content that only God knows how*
> *we're serving, no one can really*
> *take advantage of us.*

✟ MAKING SERVICE A VITAL PART
OF LIFE TOGETHER

How can a married couple develop the discipline of service? The possibilities are endless, but here are some ideas to get you started.

The service of hospitality. Peter clearly lays out for us one important way we can exercise, as a couple, the discipline of service: "Cheerfully share your home with those who need a meal or a place to stay for the night" (1 Pet. 4:9). Some people have this gift—and they're always sharing their home with others. One month it's missionaries home on furlough. Another month it's a single man or woman trying to find a job and housing. Other times it's someone else's overflow of relatives or a visiting minister or speaker. For these hospitable people, sharing their home is more of a natural gift than a discipline. But they serve as good examples for those of us who need to develop hospitality as a discipline. We do well to watch them and ask questions: How do you make a person feel comfortable away from home? How do you handle meal time, storage space, helping them get around town? What special touches in their room are particularly helpful and encouraging?

You may be thinking about opening your home to a Bible study group or perhaps to people who are in need. Whatever you choose to do, do it together before the Lord, asking God to enable you to do what you cannot do on your own and to help you feel comfortable about what you are uncomfortable doing. It is important that you and your spouse talk together about how you are going to do this. It is also important to listen carefully to some of the reasons why one or both of you may be hesitant about doing this. Remember, the discipline of service involves a choice and often requires us to do something that doesn't come naturally to us. Does she worry that her house has to be immaculate? Is he afraid he'll be expected to entertain nonstop? Talking with other people about these issues can be helpful and make your choice a more confident one. Above all, make certain both of you are in agreement. Having other people in your home really requires "extra" on your part, and if the two of you don't work together, it can be a disaster rather than a service.

The service of small things. Since this is a partnership between you as a couple and God, there is really nothing that is "small." But from the human standpoint, there are a lot of small things that need to be done. Dorcas is an example of someone who practiced the discipline of service in the small things. In Acts 9:36, we are told that she was "a believer who was always doing kind things for others, especially for the poor." When she died, weeping widows gathered in her room, "showing one another the coats and other garments Dorcas had made for them" (verse 39).

She isn't mentioned in the Bible because of her acts of service; they are merely a means of identifying her. She is mentioned because, through Peter, God raised her from the dead. We don't know very much about her, but my guess is she went back to doing little, kind things for others, just as before. You might include in your prayer together each day, "God, bring into our lives someone today whom we can serve in some small but significant way."

One of the small ways in which we can serve others can have some very big results; that is the service of guarding the reputation of another person, especially a person in leadership. Paul tells Titus to "remind your people. . . . They must not speak evil of anyone" (Titus 3:1-2). It takes discipline to refrain from entering into the gossip regarding someone's troubles or some leader's failure. It is a service that is rendered unto the Lord, and as we exercise this discipline in this way, we are strengthening not only our marriage but also the body of Christ.

The service of hiddenness. Many times, our acts of service are supposed to go unnoticed. Jesus suggested that "when you do a kindness to someone, do it secretly—don't tell your left hand what your right hand is doing" (Matt. 6:3). What are some areas of service you could participate in together where only the two of you would know you are doing it? The real joy comes when only God and the two of you know about it.

Some time ago I served someone in this way—in hiddenness. There was an incredible satisfaction that came from serving in secret. But I also noticed that later there was a strong desire to tell someone. I told Jan, but I've noticed several times since that I wanted to say something about what I did; I had to make the choice not to tell about my service.

This is a wonderful kind of service to do as a couple—at least you can tell each other! There is also a close bond that comes from the secret you share as you plan and carry out the plan. But resist the desire afterward to tell anyone else—let it be your secret together. We grow spiritually when we can enjoy doing worthy things apart from the reward of human praise or appreciation.

Being served. It's much easier to serve others than to let them serve you. I struggled with this when I started preaching, years ago. After the sermon, the preacher always went to the door of the church to greet people. One time someone had been really touched by something I'd said. As she was expressing her gratitude to me, I felt very uncomfortable. I awkwardly told her to give thanks to God for speaking to her heart. Fortunately, she was older and wiser than I was, and she leaned a little closer to me and said, "I already have, but I also wanted to thank you."

My struggle with "being served" reminded me somewhat of what Peter must have struggled with when Jesus prepared to wash Peter's feet. We noted in an earlier chapter that Peter was the only disciple who is recorded as protesting and telling Jesus—who was performing the act of a slave—that he would not allow him to wash his feet. When Jesus warned Peter that unless he let him wash his feet, Peter couldn't be his partner, Peter, in his typical exuberant way said, in essence, "In that case, give me a bath!" (see John 13:6-9). That evening, Peter learned an important lesson in receiving, in being served.

What I realized that Sunday morning, years ago, was that when we protest about someone serving us, we take away from them the opportunity to be a servant. More recently, Jan and I have struggled with this in relation to our grown children. When we go out to eat together, we just assume that we are buying since we are the parents. What we overlook is that they are now adults, and sometimes they want to give to us.

Think about this kind of service in terms of how you respond as a couple when someone gives you an unexpected gift. Are you embarrassed, thinking you have to have something to give in return? Are you embarrassed by your partner's embarrassment? Do you protest to the point where you almost destroy the other person's joy in giving to you? If so, then exercising together the discipline of service by letting others serve you may be an important growth experience for you.

Bearing one another's burdens. We are to "share each other's troubles and problems, and so obey our Lord's command. If anyone thinks he is too great to stoop to this, he is fooling himself. He is really a nobody" (Gal. 6:2-3). Those are strong words! In fact, it is this type of injunction in the Scripture that connects us with the discipline of service as opposed to self-centered service. When it comes to the service of bearing one another's burdens, we choose to respond as an act of obedience. God calls us to help our brothers and sisters bear their heavy burdens. This can be very draining, even when we are dependent on the Holy Spirit. This is why it is helpful to do this together as a couple.

As a counselor it is my job to do this for others. People make appointments with me to come to my office so that I can help them bear their burdens and problems. When I do this in my office, it is not a discipline of service; it is my vocation. But when Jan and I share together with another couple and walk with them through some dark time in their life, we are exercising the discipline of service. We also know the importance of this kind of service because we have been on the receiving end, as others have helped us carry our burdens and have shared our troubles and problems.

The ministry of prayer. Sometimes we are called to a ministry of prayer. For example, we know of a couple who has taken on the responsibility of being prayer warriors on behalf of a young man in their church who is struggling with a past full of abuse. Sometimes they have taken time between worship services on Sunday to pray with him. They are sensitive to his reactions during worship; if he is overwhelmed and leaves in tears, they follow him out, sit with him as he cries, and pray with him.

In Colossians 4:12-13 we read of Epaphras, "a servant of Christ Jesus, [who] sends you his love. He is always earnestly praying for you, asking God to make you strong and perfect and to help you know his will in everything you do." Then Paul adds, "I can assure you that he has worked hard for you with his prayers, and also for the Christians in Laodicea and Hierapolis." Epaphras had a ministry of prayer.

Service of the shared Word. One of the things Jan and I have really enjoyed over the recent years is speaking together publicly. We've done it long enough now that it looks easy to an outsider. It wasn't easy when we started, and it still isn't easy—it really is a discipline. Whenever we do a couples' retreat or speak at some other event, we struggle with each other over what we are going to do. But once we start, it is pure joy. We have fun speaking together.

You may feel led as a couple to teach a home Bible study together. Do it. It will require work, but it is a wonderful way to exercise the discipline of service together. There are a variety of ways you can do it together. Some actually team teach, others take turns doing alternate sessions. Some couples we know choose to have the husband lead and the wife add to what he says. Another couple chooses to have the wife lead, and the husband helps in the preparation. However you choose to work together, the service of the shared Word is a very rewarding discipline for a couple.

HOW SERVICE CAN MAKE
YOUR MARRIAGE BETTER

The discipline of service is beneficial to a marriage in that it helps us get beyond ourselves—and beyond our own marriage. Sometimes we feel that our own relationship needs to be "OK" before we have anything to offer other people. Many couples are so self-absorbed that they become paralyzed. If we serve when, even as a couple, we're not "OK," we are even more dependent on the Holy Spirit to work in us and through us.

This discipline must be chosen and practiced with discernment, and sometimes, depending on where the problems in our own marriage lie, a certain type of service may not be the best choice. But to follow Christ together means that we are servants. Being servants together can multiply our effectiveness in the lives of other people. And it builds something that neither one of us can do alone; in this way, service can bind us closer together as a

*If we serve when, even as a couple, we're not "OK,"
we are even more dependent on the Holy Spirit
to work in us and through us.*

couple—it is one more experience that is not "yours" or "mine," but "ours."

TO TALK ABOUT TOGETHER

- In what ways have you and your spouse encountered barriers to serving others? Do you compete with each other? Does one of you prefer working alone?
- What distinguishes an action as a discipline of service rather than simply being an act of love? What are you doing as a couple that would be called "acts of love"? What are you doing that would be called "disciplines of service"?
- What areas of service would you like to be involved with as a couple? Individually make lists and then compare them. Talk about the differences and how you might choose one thing and begin on it together.

Confessing to One Another:
Why It's Necessary, How It Works

PAUL and Julie had been separated for more than six months. I checked for all the obvious reasons they might be separated. They kept saying that they loved each other, but they just couldn't live with each other anymore. Paul was the most vocal of the two on that point, but they both agreed. So now I was curious as to what made it so impossible for them to live together.

It didn't take long to find out. As I started to press for more information, Julie suddenly took over the conversation. She was angry about the separation, and she talked heatedly for more than twenty minutes, letting both Paul and me know how she felt.

As she talked, I watched Paul almost literally shrink into the corner of the couch. He got very quiet, and when it was clear to Julie that he had stopped listening, she finally stopped talking. Suddenly Paul was back and said, "See? That's what I can't live with! She's impossible!"

I asked Paul if he disagreed with anything Julie had said. He thought for a moment and said, "No, not really. But the problem is more how she says it than what she says." Then I asked Paul if he could tell me what the real issue was for Julie—what was behind all the anger and animation as she talked? He tried a couple of times to summarize what he thought she was saying to him, but by the third attempt, Julie started in on him again. "He never gets it! That's what's so frustrating. No matter how many times, or how many ways I tell him, he never gets the point."

I decided to see if *I* had gotten the point. As I attempted to help Paul by summarizing for him what I had heard Julie say, she started to relax. Then her eyes filled with tears as I asked her if I had heard her correctly. Now there was a whole different Julie in the room. She was vulnerable and open. Paul noticed also and responded warmly to her. I commented on the change, and through her tears she told both of us how desperately she wanted Paul to hear her heart, not just her words. Then she started telling Paul about how afraid she was, especially when he left. She admitted that she was hard to live with but then told Paul how she longed for him to understand her and help make it feel safer for her in the marriage.

Now it was Paul who changed. He didn't withdraw into the couch anymore. Instead, he sat forward and reached out for Julie's hand. As he did, he told her how whenever she used that harsh, angry voice with him he felt as if he had been a bad little boy and was just waiting to be punished. "I lived like that all my childhood—I don't want to live that way as an adult." The rest of the conversation was very moving as both Julie and Paul listened to one another's heart, perhaps for the first time since before their wedding.

What made the difference? The situation changed, partly because I was able to add some things to what Julie had said by guessing what she was feeling on the inside. And it wasn't anger; it was fear. By doing this, I was helping Julie "confess" to Paul what was really going on inside her. And as Paul heard Julie's heart, he "confessed" to her what was really going on inside him. Together, they experienced the discipline of *confession*.

To Whom Do We Confess?

One of the definitions Webster gives for "confess" is "to own or admit as true."[1] This comes closest to what is meant by the Greek word translated "confess," which literally means "my words are in agreement with what is." The two things—the words and what the words are connected to—are the same thing. If I am confessing to being rude, then my words will be in agreement with my rude behavior. In Julie and Paul's case, they "confessed" to each other when their words agreed with what was really going on inside each of them.

The discipline of confession has an interesting history. In the early church, the principle was described in James 5:16, which says, "Admit your faults to one another and pray for each other so that you may be healed." In the early fellowship, people confessed to one another. Over time, confession became more formal. Perhaps the early church found that some people couldn't be trusted with listening to someone else's confession, so certain people were given the task of listening to confessions. Eventually this role was given to those in leadership, and priests became the ones to whom people confessed their faults.

This too was abused by some, so that the leaders of the Reformation decided that confession should be redirected—to God only. You didn't need a priest to listen and pronounce forgiveness; you could go directly to God and bypass the priest. Because of the finished work of Christ, no other mediator was necessary. This is what many of us do today. If we sin, we take it directly to God and ask forgiveness. And that is our privilege and right as believers.

But what do we do with James 5:16? Is it obsolete? It can't be, for it is part of God's Word. Somehow we need to recapture this discipline of confession and find the balance, knowing that we can come directly into God's presence and "confess our sins to

1. *Webster's College Dictionary* (New York: Random House, 1991).

him, [for] he can be depended on to forgive us and to cleanse us from every wrong" (1 John 1:9). But we are also to confess our sins to "one another and pray for each other so that [we] may be healed" (James 5:16).

WHAT DO WE CONFESS?

This is an important question. We might think that we are supposed to confess the worst things first—and, if that is the case, forget it! It is helpful, instead, to think of confession as covering a whole continuum of topics. At one end of the continuum will be things that may be scary to confess, but at least we know that they won't cause us to be cut off or rejected. It may be something we are struggling with, such as pride, or holding a grudge against someone. We may be struggling in a relationship with our boss or with a coworker. These are not easy to share with our spouse, but they are "here-and-now" issues that will be easier to deal with together.

Toward the middle of the continuum might be some of the "sins done to me." In the Lord's prayer, Jesus said we should include these words, "and forgive us our sins, just as we have forgiven those who have sinned against us" (Matt. 6:12). There are two types of sins—those we commit, and those that have been committed against us. All of us have been sinned against in some way, and confessing those kinds of things to our mate is a part of the discipline of confession.

On the other end of the continuum are the sins we have committed. We need to examine why we want to confess these sins, for sometimes we simply want to shift the burden off our shoulders and onto someone else's. Sometimes I am so overwhelmed with my guilt over some wrong I have done that I just have to "get it off my chest." But then it is on someone else's chest, and maybe they didn't want it. Perhaps you've had the experience where a friend has confessed something to you, and as you think about it later you wonder why he or she told you. There simply was no context in which to understand their confession.

The sins we have committed are probably the most difficult things to confess, and we need to understand the implications of confessing some of these sins. It's not that we should avoid them. We just need to have a context of confession that begins on the other side of the continuum before moving to this side.

When we think about confessing our sins to "one another" when the other is our spouse, we can clearly see why this is a discipline. I have yet to meet a husband and wife who find it easy to confess their faults to each other. The reasons are many. No one knows us better than our spouse—and no one knows better the things we are in denial about. We can deceive ourselves, but seldom can we deceive the one with whom we live. No one is exempt from the truth that "the heart is the most deceitful thing there is and desperately wicked" (Jer. 17:9).

To avoid deceiving ourselves, it is important to consider the

---

No one knows us better than our spouse—and no one knows better the things we are in denial about.

---

kind of instrument we use to measure our life. The reference point we use will often determine the kinds of problems we uncover. Left to ourselves, we will often use a faulty guideline, making it impossible to make an accurate assessment. Perhaps I use that faulty guideline because it doesn't disturb some problems I want left covered. For instance, my faulty guideline might be the belief that emotions are inferior to rational thinking. If I am rude or tactless to someone, I do not see that as something I need to confess, for to me the other person is simply being too emotional. The problem lies with him or her, rather than with me. All of us come out of family systems that have their own unwritten rules, and some of them aren't biblical! That's why we always need to be opening ourselves to God's Word and principles. When we develop the discipline of confession together, we can help one another see the truth of Scripture and get away from the faulty guidelines we've picked up in our lives. Confession helps us to stay accountable—to one another and to God. And because God is a part of our process, he provides the only accurate plumb line—his Word.

All of us come out of family systems that have their own unwritten rules, and some of them aren't biblical!

✝ MAKING CONFESSION A VITAL PART
OF LIFE TOGETHER

The discipline of confession in our marriage is built on mutual trust. Most of us have a problem trusting someone else. When these trust issues enter into your marriage, they make it very difficult for you to exercise this discipline. However, confession and trust can build each other within the marriage. This is a time for real sensitivity to one another. Husband and wife need to demonstrate that they can be trusted—not to discount the other's pain or difficulty, not to judge, not to break a confidence. Be sure to work together to set your guidelines for this exercise. Here are some basic guidelines we've found to be effective.

Listen. When your spouse is "confessing" to you—working on making what he says match everything he is experiencing—your most important task is to *listen.* That may sound obvious, even simplistic, but it is always where confession must begin. While most people think that good communication requires learning how to talk, the real key is learning how to listen.

Here's an exercise to help you with your listening skills. First, stop thinking about what you are going to say in response to what your mate is sharing. When he or she stops talking, say, "Let me see if I understand you," and paraphrase what you think he or she has just said. Allow yourself to be corrected. This isn't a test; it's an exercise in listening. After your spouse has corrected your interpretation, say again, "Let me see if I understand you correctly," and then paraphrase again what you have just heard. Continue to do this until your spouse says, "Yes, that's what I'm trying to say." When this has been established, you are free to respond to what has been said. But take your time. Be sure that your words agree with what is going on inside of you.

Be quiet. Being quiet is especially important when you feel confused or you can't say something supportive. There are positive ways to be quiet, and there are negative ways to be quiet. Here are some of the positive ways.

Stay with your husband or wife, physically. Don't choose your quiet time to go to the bathroom. As you are being quiet, perhaps you may want to say, "Let me think a bit about what you said." Touch your spouse, even as you are quiet and thinking. Touch lets a person know you are still present and involved. In your silence, try to understand what your spouse is feeling, and try to imagine what is behind some of the obvious emotions he or she is displaying.

If your spouse begins to talk while you are being quiet, go back to listening. Allow about five or ten minutes of quiet before you respond with your own thoughts about what has been shared with you.

One of the things I often do that shuts down confession on the spot is to not only talk too soon, but to try to be "helpful." As Jan shares something with me, I want to jump in and show her how she can really conquer that problem. I think I am being supportive, but her silence tells me very quickly that I am anything but supportive. I need to *be quiet* and continue to listen.

Don't pry. One sure way to close down confession is to try to force the other person to go beyond what he or she wants to say. We tend to pry by asking too many questions, or by saying things that begin with, "You only feel that way because . . . ," and we fill in the rest with our own ideas. Let the other person determine how much will be shared and where he or she wants to stop.

Pray silently. There are several things to be praying for as you

---

One sure way to close down confession is to try to force the other person to go beyond what he or she wants to say.

---

listen. You may want to pray that your spouse will sense your concern and your interest in what is being said. You also need to pray for insight and understanding as you listen. Often, as I am listening to a couple in my office, such as Paul and Julie, I am praying that God will help me understand what is really being said and that he will give me insight into what needs to be done in response. When Jan or I do that with each other, our serious conversations are much more effective.

Keep confidences. Remember that what your spouse shares with you is now your secret. The "your" is plural, referring to only you and your mate. An important part of trust is knowing that what you share with each other never goes beyond the other unless you both agree to share it with someone else. If your mate shares something personal with you, you do not have the right to share it with someone else unless your spouse gives permission. If you can remember this and practice it, you will strengthen your partner's ability to trust you.

How does a couple go about developing this important discipline? Here is what Jan and I—and other couples—have learned.

Commit yourselves to having a set time every week just for the two of you. This is not a "date night." It will probably work better at either breakfast or lunch. The agenda for this time together is just to be together. It is a time to check in with each other. Jan and I, for many years, reserved Friday morning breakfasts for each other. We would head to a restaurant on the beach and often sit there for several hours. Sometimes it was a time of mutual confession about ourselves; other times we would plan our schedules for the coming month. Sometimes we simply sat and enjoyed the ocean. But it provided an opportunity for us to develop some of these disciplines together.

Begin with some of your childhood and adolescent memories, specifically some of the "sins done to you." It might help for you to make notes about specific periods in your growing-up years. Take an hour and reminisce, writing down things that happened to you as you recall them. Then talk with your spouse about your memories. Talk about not only the events but what you remember thinking and feeling at the time. After you've done this several times, you can talk about some of the more hurtful memories.

After you feel more comfortable doing the first two exercises, begin to talk with each other about some of the "here-and-now" issues. Talk about situations in which you feel fearful or anxious. Talk about some of the people who intimidate you, speculating on why you relate to them this way. Talk about some of your fears and dreams about the future. Remember, confession is verbally agreeing with what is going on in your life at this present moment. Invite your spouse into your inner life.

You may want to consider meeting with some other couples in order to be mutually supportive of each other's marriages. If several couples want to meet together for this purpose, talk to them about the importance of confession. It is important to remember that things you confess to each other as a couple need to be cleared with the other person before you share it with anyone else, including a small group. But there can be real strength and support when couples can be honest with each other about their personal issues and can support each other before the Lord.

HOW CONFESSION CAN MAKE
YOUR MARRIAGE BETTER

As difficult as it can be to carry out, the act of confession really does cleanse us and make us more fit to function, both as individuals and as a couple. We have noticed several benefits that accompany this discipline.

The Discipline of Confession Leads Us to a Renewed Sense of Freedom

All of us struggle to make peace in our own hearts. We want to break what feels like an internal bondage to some secret part of ourselves. In the midst of the struggle, we often lose sight of our mate—or we even lose touch with him or her. When we are confronted about our distance and withdrawal, we may deny our behavior or try to explain ourselves. But we know the truth: "For down in their hearts they know right from wrong. God's laws are written within them; their own conscience accuses them, or sometimes excuses them" (Rom. 2:12-13).

John came to see me because he was having trouble concentrating at work. As we talked, it became clear that he had an oversensitive conscience. He was convinced that he was a horrible person, and he spent most of his energy in a self-absorbed self-examination that left little room for anyone else. I asked him if his wife knew how much he struggled with his view of himself. "Oh no!" he exclaimed. "No one knows. You're the first person I've told." We talked about the possibility of bringing his wife in so we could talk together about his concerns. Finally he agreed, and when he confessed to his wife how obsessed he was about his failings, she replied warmly, "John, I know you struggle. But I've prayed and prayed that you would talk to me about it, and you've always resisted. I'm so glad you could finally say these things to me." John sat there stunned for a moment and then said, "Wow! I can't believe I told her. I feel a sense of hope finally. I feel freer."

Confession is the only way to stop this internal struggle. When we can agree with God about ourselves and admit our faults, our struggles, and our fears to our partner, we can begin to relax. There is no freedom without confession. *What a relief it is to finally give up the weight of our excuses.* "Confession alone makes deep fellowship possible, and the lack of it explains much of the superficial quality"[2] we struggle against in so many of our relationships, especially within our marriage.

Confession Helps Us Avoid Sin

What a relief it is to finally give up
the weight of our excuses.

In a very real sense, whatever is unconfessed in our lives still owns us. The things that are hidden have control over us. Proverbs 28:13 says, "A man who refuses to admit his mistakes can never be successful. But if he confesses and forsakes them, he gets

2. Dallas Willard, *The Spirit of the Disciplines* (San Francisco: Harper, 1988), 188.

another chance." In this proverb, there is a connection between confessing and forsaking. This can be seen clearly in some very practical ways.

For example, during counseling sessions I have heard a husband

---

Whatever is unconfessed in our lives still owns us.

---

or a wife confess some weakness. Later on, when I check with them about how they are doing, almost invariably the problem has diminished in its intensity and may have even ceased to be a problem. Bringing what was hidden in darkness out into the light through confession breaks the power of the hidden secret.

Confession Brings Us Closer, Not Only to Each Other But Also to God
I vividly remember occasions on which I've shared with Jan areas of struggle I had previously kept to myself because I was afraid or ashamed to talk about them. But once the hidden was brought out into the open, I became aware that a distance had been built up between us by my secrecy. After talking about it, we felt closer. Even when the subject of the discussion is upsetting to one or both of us, we are together in the concern—we are on the same side, and we have a common goal. Some of our closest times have been when one or the other of us has confessed to being fearful or hurt by someone or struggling with something. There is a sense of mutuality that results in a greater sense of closeness.

Sometimes when we confess something to the other person, it can lead to a meaningful time of prayer together. Thus the discipline of confession enriches the discipline of prayer, and vice versa.

Confession Helps Us Grow
Jeremiah says, "You can't heal a wound by saying it's not there!" (6:14). The first step of healing is to acknowledge the wound; the first step of growth is to acknowledge our needs. If you think of

confession as bringing something out of darkness into light, the analogy with growth can be very obvious. Very little grows in darkness. Nearly everything in life requires light for growth. What is true in the natural world is just as true in the spiritual realm. When confession brings things out of the darkness into the light, growth can take place.

Bob had been talking with me about his problem with lust and fantasizing about other women. As we talked about some of the reasons for his behaviors, he began to see that his secret inner life of fantasy was a barrier to his feeling close to his wife. "I think your secret thought life is a way you protect yourself from intimacy," I suggested. His first response was to agree, and then he disagreed. But gradually he saw how he was avoiding the very intimacy and closeness he claimed to desire. It was only when he could begin to confess what was going on inside his mind that he was able to see that the issues of lust and fantasy were his way of avoiding the growth that was needed in his life and marriage.

Confession Leads to Confession.

Years ago, when I was first learning about principles of confession, I decided to go out on a limb and tell Jan about something from my childhood that I had never shared with anyone. Part of me was afraid she would respond negatively, but to my surprise, she also shared something very personal with me. My ability to confess to her led her to do the same with me. Confession can lead to mutual self-disclosure. And that leads to a greater sense of intimacy with each other.

TO TALK ABOUT TOGETHER

- What is your "trust quotient"? Do you trust too easily? Do you find it difficult to trust anyone? Whom do you trust, and whom can you talk to when it comes to personal fears and failures?

- Discuss a time you could set aside for just the two of you. Can you make a commitment to that time being reserved for each other? What would help you make that commitment?
- Describe some things your mate does that help you trust him or her. Review the suggestions under "How Confession Can Make Your Marriage Better." Which of these suggestions would be most helpful in building a trusting environment together?
- Think of an area of sin in your life that would be more manageable if you could talk to someone early on—when the temptation begins. How might you help one another confess your weakness before it leads to sin? Talk about how you might incorporate this kind of care into your times of prayer, either individually or together.

ELEVEN

The Power of Forgiveness:
God's Grace to Move beyond the Hurt

RAY and Elaine were in their early fifties. They came to see me because Ray had had an affair five years earlier. According to Ray, they finally came to counseling because "Elaine just can't get over what I did." Elaine responded matter-of-factly, "Of course I could get over it. But first I have to understand why." As she went on to expound upon her remark, it was easy to see where the counseling would need to begin.

For their first five or six meetings, Elaine went over every piece of data she had been able to gather in her effort to understand Ray's failure in their marriage. At one point, Ray commented that every time they were alone together, Elaine asked more questions. "Somewhere in the midst of the endless questions," he added, "she usually asks me if I've had any further insight into why I did what I did. It never seems to end." He continued, "No matter how much she knows, she still doesn't know enough to understand. Why, several years ago she even took the other woman out for lunch and asked her questions for two hours."

One time I asked Ray why he stayed in the marriage. It was obvious to all of us that there certainly wasn't much enjoyment in the relationship for either of them at this point. After thinking a moment, he said, "I've wondered that myself many times, but I never really wanted to leave the marriage. I just did something stupid five years ago, and I guess part of me figures this is the way I pay for what I did."

I never was able to help Elaine figure out Ray's behavior. At least not to her satisfaction. I added some additional information about Ray's fears of closeness and how he used the other relationship to keep himself from feeling overwhelmed emotionally by Elaine. We even looked back at some of his early family experiences to support some of the new information.

Elaine finally called a halt to the counseling. I think it was because I was starting to press her for what her plans were once she understood the "why." She avoided my question several times, but finally answered, "I guess I'll have to forgive him." I could tell she didn't like my pressing her for reasons why she couldn't just forgive Ray—even without a full understanding of his motivations and problems. Finally she said angrily, "If I forgive him, then it's too easy. What's to keep him from doing it again?" That's when she stopped the counseling. What neither she nor Ray was able to see was that as long as she withheld forgiveness, she was in control.

As long as she withheld forgiveness,
she was in control.

I've thought about Ray and Elaine often in the years since and wondered if anything ever changed in their marriage. I'd hate to think she was still asking questions in order to understand. I also think of this couple whenever another couple is sitting with me and for some obscure reason one of them refuses to forgive the other for something hurtful. Some of them end the marriage be-

cause, in their words, "This is just something I can't forgive!"
When this happens, it is clear that the discipline of forgiveness
has not been a part of their marriage.

OUR STRUGGLE WITH FORGIVENESS

It's not uncommon for couples to struggle with understanding forgiveness as a discipline. Part of the problem is that
we haven't really tried to understand forgiveness from God's perspective and define it according to God's understanding. Even the
disciples, as they listened to Jesus teach on the subject, had problems understanding God's point of view regarding forgiveness.

One day, after Jesus had been teaching on the importance of
dealing with people who harm us, Peter asked, "Sir, how often
should I forgive a brother who sins against me? Seven times?"
(Matt. 18:21). Peter was being extremely generous with his offer
of seven times, for the common teaching of the rabbis of that day
was that we only had to forgive three times, sort of a "three
strikes and you're out" approach to forgiveness. So when Peter offered that he could forgive seven times, he was going way beyond
the common wisdom of his day. Jesus' response must have
shocked him: "No! Seventy times seven!" One of the early manu-
script copies of Matthew has a notation that adds the words "a
day" to the "seventy times seven." That wouldn't have made
much difference, for Jesus' admonition to forgive 490 times was
so far beyond the thinking of that day that his point was clear:
There is to be no limit to our forgiving.

Following this exchange, Jesus told the disciples a parable
about a man who owes a king a huge debt. After the king forgives
the debt, this same man goes out and tries to collect a small debt
from a friend. When his friend can't pay, the man has him
thrown into jail. When the king finds out, he brings the man
back into his presence and calls him an "evil-hearted wretch!"

(verse 32) and then makes this important point: "Shouldn't you have mercy on others, just as I had mercy on you?" (verse 33). Jesus was saying that someone who has been forgiven so much himself must have a very generous spirit of forgiveness toward others.

A Debt We Cannot Pay

It's easy to see his point until we realize that each of us is like the man in the parable; we've been forgiven a debt we cannot pay. The debt we owe for our sin requires our death. But Jesus paid our debt, so when God looks at his records and comes to our name, written across the page are the words, "This debt is forgiven! Nothing owed!"

Paul describes this process of forgiveness in Colossians 2:13-14. "He forgave all your sins, and blotted out the charges proved against you, the list of his commandments which you had not obeyed. He took this list of sins and destroyed it by nailing it to Christ's cross." God took our debt—the debt we owe because of our sins—and canceled it by nailing it to the cross! That's forgiveness!

Look again at Ray and Elaine. Elaine felt, and justifiably so, that Ray owed her something. He had betrayed her and violated her trust and their marriage vows. He should pay something for that. But how? He cannot undo what he has already done. And nothing less than the undoing of his sinful act can satisfy the debt. Ray is in the same position as was the man in Jesus' parable—he owes a debt that cannot be paid.

All that can be done with a debt that cannot be paid is to cancel it—to forgive the offense. But, as Elaine herself said, "I can't just forgive him. It was too terrible a thing for him to do!" All true, except for the fact that Elaine is also the man in the parable. She owes a debt she cannot pay, and the King of Glory has forgiven her her unpayable debt. She, too, is to show the same mercy that has been shown her by God. She is to forgive out of the forgiveness God has already extended to her.[1]

In the movie *The Prince of Tides,* the lead character, Tom Wingo, is about to reveal to his sister's counselor some horrible secret from within his family. His mother pleads with him not to tell, but as he walks away to leave, he turns back and assures his mother that "nothing ever happens in families that is beyond forgiveness." When I heard that line, I thought to myself, "Wow! That's biblical!" And the same is true in marriage—nothing ever happens in a marriage that is beyond forgiveness. Why? Because, out of God's forgiveness toward us we can forgive the sins that others commit against us.

FORGIVENESS: FOUR MISPERCEPTIONS

We have acquired some big misperceptions about forgiveness, and each of them makes forgiveness easier to avoid and more difficult to practice.

If I Forgive, I Will Make Right the Wrong the Other Person Has Done

When we reverse this and *seek* forgiveness, we know that forgiveness does not make our wrong action right, nor does it excuse us. In the same way, when we forgive others of the wrongs they have committed against us, we do not excuse what they have done. We simply recognize that we have been hurt unjustly, and then we turn the matter over to God. Forgiving frees us so that we can begin healing. Further, when we take this misperception and apply it to God, we can easily see that it is not true. In forgiving sin, God does not make sin suddenly acceptable. Sin remains sin; only now it is forgiven.

Sometimes we want to hold on to something hurtful our

1. The author has an expanded discussion of this in his book *Forgiving Our Parents, Forgiving Ourselves* (Ann Arbor: Servant Publications, 1991).

spouse has done to us because we believe that if we forgive, we are giving our spouse permission to hurt us again. At one point, Elaine said to Ray that she was afraid that if she forgave him for his affair, he would think it was no big deal and do it again. If there is any basis to that fear, the problem is not with the spouse's act of forgiveness, but with the person being forgiven. His or her sin may be an outgrowth of some inner compulsion, addiction, or simply an inability to empathize with the pain he or she has caused.

Forgiveness Must Be Instant

We often buy into this misperception because we know that 1 John 1:9 assures us that whenever we confess our sin, God forgives our sin. How long does it take? Instantly it's done! In our efforts to be Christlike, we sometimes believe that whenever we need to forgive, we must do so quickly.

What we forget is that God, in the bigger picture, was never in a hurry to forgive. Think about when sin first entered the human race—the Garden of Eden. When is forgiveness complete? When our certificate of debt is nailed to the cross. What took place over the thousands of years between the Garden of Eden and the Cross? God was in the process of forgiving, but he was in no hurry. Why? Because he wanted each of us to know that he takes sin seriously. Forgiveness is no light matter!

One day Ron called me in a panic to make an appointment. He had just found out that his wife, Barbara, had been having an affair with his best friend. We set a time, and Ron and his wife came into my office. I started the session by saying something to Ron about his hurt and anger toward Barbara. He quickly pointed out that he was "over all that stuff." Knowing he had only found out about the affair three days earlier, I expressed some surprise that he was over these feelings. He made it clear to me that because he was a Christian, he had forgiven his wife for what she had done. When I agreed with his need to forgive and then said something about the recency of the pain, he reemphasized his earlier point about being a Christian, and that what they wanted to do was strengthen their marriage so that this kind of thing wouldn't happen again.

When he called me a couple of days later to tell me that Barbara had left again, I talked with him about the danger of forgiving too quickly. Quick forgiveness can be interpreted by the other person as meaning "no big deal," which for some can be an invitation to continue the hurtful behavior.

Quick forgiveness can be interpreted by the other person as meaning "no big deal."

Obviously, the time to forgive lies somewhere between the way that Ron forgave and the way that Elaine kept putting off forgiveness. One could add to the words of Ecclesiastes that there is a "time to forgive, and a time to wait to forgive." *The important thing is that we are always moving in the direction of forgiving.*

We were with some friends recently for a day, and early in the day, the husband did something that hurt his wife's feelings. When he asked for her forgiveness, she said, "No, not now." He responded by asking, "What time will the forgiveness come?" When she said, after reflecting a moment, "Oh, around five o'clock this afternoon," Jan and I both looked at each other and wondered what the rest of the day would be like. But things went along smoothly, and at five o'clock that afternoon he asked his wife for the promised forgiveness, which now was freely given. They both understood the need for an appropriate amount of time to heal from the hurt but also knew that closure through forgiveness was essential.

If I Forgive, Then I Must Also Forget

Sometimes, when I can't forget, I then assume I have not really forgiven. We often struggle with this misperception in our desire to be more Christlike; we believe we should be able to forgive the same way God forgives. And since when God forgives he also forgets, we should be able to do the same.

But we are different from God. One of the reasons we remember past hurts is to protect ourselves from being hurt in the same way again. We need to learn something through our forgiveness, so we need to remember. God has no need to learn anything, for he knows everything already. Therefore, there is no need for him to remember.

Elaine and I talked about this in one of our sessions. She felt that if she forgave Ray, she would have to forget that he had betrayed her and their vows. "I have to remember," she said with a sense of urgency, "because I can never let him hurt me like that ever again! So since I won't let myself forget, I guess I can't forgive." She understood the protective part of the remembering but never could see that she could forgive and remember at the same time.

One of the things I've found helpful when people have difficulty both forgiving and remembering is to suggest that every time they remember the hurt and the pain, they also review the process of forgiveness, not only how they have forgiven, but also how much they themselves have been forgiven by God. Turning a painful memory into a reminder of God's love and grace can effectively reduce the pain over time.

If I Forgive, Then I Must Also Reconcile

Reconciliation is different from forgiveness. I can forgive someone and never be reconciled with him or her. All the work of forgiving takes place within *me*. But in order to be reconciled with someone, both of us need to be involved in the process. For example, in the case of Ron and Barbara, Ron could work through the process of forgiving Barbara on his own. He did not need her participation in order to work through that process. But genuine reconciliation could only take place when Barbara entered into the same process as Ron, acknowledging the wrong she had done and the pain she had caused. Her failure to even consider doing either of these things, along with her failure to feel godly sorrow over her sin, meant that if Ron trusted her too quickly and reconciled with her, he was vulnerable to her hurting him again, which is exactly what happened.

We need to see forgiveness and reconciliation as two separate issues. While forgiveness is absolutely necessary, reconciliation is optional. I do have to forgive in order to experience true reconciliation. But I don't have to be reconciled in order to forgive. After all, reconciliation requires the effort of both parties, and I cannot control how the other person will respond to me. I can do everything in my power to reconcile, but the other person can fight the process and prevent reconciliation from occurring.

We need to see forgiveness and reconciliation
as two separate issues.

However, in marriage, forgiveness should always move toward reconciliation. Since, individually, we have been forgiven so much, there is nothing that can happen in a marriage that is beyond forgiveness if both people are willing to humble themselves before God and work through the process. We need to begin the process as quickly as possible, but we must also be willing to move slowly within the process, if necessary. We can and should take the time to heal, as well as to rebuild trust, so that true and lasting reconciliation can take place. Easy reconciliation, like easy forgiveness, only ends up excusing hurtful behaviors, and that leaves the door open to the continuation of those behaviors.

When Barbara came back the second time, Ron said that he wanted to forgive her, but that he was hurt and angry and he needed time to process those feelings. He also told her that he needed her to help him rebuild trust in her. She would have to be in the process with him. If she responded positively, then they would be "moving in the direction of forgiving and reconciling." If she simply ignored what Ron was saying and continued to hurt him through her behavior, then Ron's first task would be to protect himself in some way from further hurt. True forgiveness can come only when I am safe from being hurt again. True reconciliation can come only when the other person is as involved in the process as I am.

One could say that the only way reconciliation is impossible in a marriage is when one person is either too afraid to open up to the other person, or when one person has allowed his or her heart to harden to the point of being unresponsive toward God or spouse. In Ron and Barbara's case, Ron's honesty about his feelings over what Barbara had done was almost a relief to her. She knew she had been wrong in her behavior, and she also knew that Ron was hurt and angry. When he denied those feelings, she felt that he didn't really care about what she did. When he was honest with her, she felt that he really did care, and that helped her deal with what she had done.

✝ MAKING FORGIVENESS A VITAL PART
OF LIFE TOGETHER

1. *Think of forgiving as a privilege.* In many ways, forgiveness is a life-giving process, not only for the person we forgive, but also for ourselves. When Jesus met with the disciples after his resur-

rection, "he breathed on them and told them, 'Receive the Holy Spirit. If you forgive anyone's sins, they are forgiven. If you refuse to forgive them, they are unforgiven'" (John 20:22-23). We are not only entrusted with the message of forgiveness, we are living examples of God's forgiveness.

Since we have this great privilege, let's not neglect it. To begin, forgiveness needs to be tied to confession. Look back over the ways we can practice the discipline of confession as a couple, and tie into each the discipline of forgiveness. For example, as you "confess" some of the things that happened to you as a child, as an adolescent, and as an adult, your spouse can take anything you did and remind you that in Christ you are forgiven. In the same way, your mate can take any sin that was done to you during any of these periods and help you discern whether or not you have forgiven that person. If you need time to process the hurtful memory that has been buried, your partner can hold you accountable to arrive at some point in the future when you will forgive.

In the same way, whenever either one of you "confesses" something in the here and now, remind each other that this confession is done in the context of forgiveness. Remember, there is nothing in marriage that is beyond forgiveness—some things just take a little longer than others.

2. Learn to keep short accounts with each other and to help each other keep short accounts with others. A number of studies have been done that show the connection between serious, and even terminal, illnesses and our holding on to grudges against other people.[2] Simply put, it's bad for our health—physically, emotionally, and spiritually—to *not* forgive. So make a commitment to each other that you will not hold grudges. This does not mean that you forgive instantly. It does mean that you will stay in the process of moving toward forgiveness and that you will help each other do this.

2. See David Stoop, *Self-Talk* (Grand Rapids: Baker/Fleming Revell), 1981.

> *It's bad for our health—physically, emotionally, and*
> *spiritually—to not forgive.*

Try to avoid a common pitfall: When your spouse has been wronged by another person, do not try to help him or her understand the other person's motivation or even their limitations. Whenever we try to help our spouse better understand someone else's position in a disagreement, we come across as if we are defending the enemy. What I've found with Jan is that when I focus more on understanding how she is hurting and do not try to even think of the other person, she is able to come into a balance whereby she can see the other person's limitations or perspective. Whenever she perceives I am focusing on her instead of trying to get her to see the bigger picture, *she* is free to see the bigger picture. Whenever I try to help her see the bigger picture, she feels I am not on her side anymore.

3. Practice setting a time to forgive. Whenever you do something that hurts your mate, rather than your typical way of handling it, ask for forgiveness. Then, if the forgiveness is refused, ask, "Well, then, what time will the forgiveness come?" Then ask for the forgiveness when the time comes.

One principle that I believe applies to forgiveness is that the more hurtful the behavior, the more time I will need to forgive. If God could take the necessary time to work through the process of forgiveness, I need to understand and practice that principle as well. Some things can be forgiven on the spot, whereas other things may take anywhere from several hours to several months. Learn to give yourself the appropriate amount of time to work through forgiving.

4. Choose carefully the time and setting for confessing and forgiving. In the car during rush-hour traffic is not the place. In front of friends and relatives isn't either. The two of you may choose a third party both of you trust if the issue has become complicated and overwhelming to one or both of you. When one or both of you is tired or angry, decide together that now is not the time, but agree to a time soon when you can work through the problem. In this sense, we may go to bed without an issue getting resolved, but we have both made a commitment to deal with it, and we have put it in a place of high priority. In the meantime, we must suspend our arguments and judgments as best we can and pray for calmness and wisdom when the set time arrives.

HOW FORGIVENESS CAN MAKE
YOUR MARRIAGE BETTER

In all of our workshops on marriage, Jan and I have a closing session in which we describe forgiveness as the mortar that holds together the building blocks of intimacy. We don't think you can have a close, satisfying marriage unless you have learned the discipline of forgiveness. Such a marriage requires that we learn not only how to work through disagreements and conflict, but that we also learn how to repair the damage that is done in the heat of the argument. Forgiveness is an attitude that always creates within us an openness to reconciliation, and no marriage can survive without this attitude.

TO TALK ABOUT TOGETHER

- Which of the four misperceptions about forgiveness have you heard espoused by someone? Do you agree that they are untrue? Why or why not?
- What is your personal reaction to the statement that "nothing ever happens in a marriage that is beyond forgiveness"?

- How long does it take you, on the inside, to forgive your spouse for different infractions? Talk about the time you need and how you can help each other in this area.

TWELVE

Money and Marriage:
Becoming a Giving Team

TOM and Jenny probably had more money than anyone with whom I had ever spent significant time. At least they made it appear that way. They lived in a massive house on the seashore in southern California. They used limousines to go everywhere except for those short trips around town. Tom had a wad of bills in his pocket at all times that included at least twenty-five or thirty hundred-dollar bills. He had built a huge company and seldom needed to go to the office anymore. But he still dressed for the office and looked like he stepped off the pages of a men's fashion magazine. I met them when they came to me for marriage counseling.

As we talked, Jenny made it clear that she enjoyed some of the perks of their lifestyle, but she was fed up. Her monthly allowance was less than what Tom had in his pocket. If she spent any money beyond her allowance, it was World War III at their house. If she asked any question at all about their financial condition, Tom flew into a rage and left the house. One time, Jenny said that even though they were both Christians, they never

153

gave anything to the church or any other Christian organization. "But we have our favorite charities," she said, and went on to list them. "Tom and I are very involved, and we have made so many friends through these organizations." Tom was hardly aware of what she had just said.

A couple of sessions later, Tom walked out in the middle of a session after angrily declaring to both Jenny and me that he had provided a good lifestyle for her and the kids and he wasn't about to do more than he was doing. Then he added that Jenny had no need to know anything more about the way he handled their finances. It was obvious that in their household money was power, and whoever had control of the money had the power. Tom was in control—and he planned to keep it that way!

It was obvious that in their household money was power, and whoever had control of the money had the power.

In my mind, I was comparing Tom and Jenny's attitude toward money with that of Jim and Renee. I met with them after Jim lost the family electronics business through some deceptive actions of one of his most trusted assistants. Prior to losing the business, they had lived very well. No one envied what they had, for they shared freely with others. Jim and Renee were also known for their generous support, not only of the church but also of other Christian organizations in the area. They enjoyed what they had, and, most of all, they just loved to give.

When they lost everything, including their large country estate with room for several horses, I saw more struggle in people who knew them than I did in Jim and Renee themselves. One man said to me, "I thought God was supposed to protect your money if you were faithful in tithing. With what's happened to Jim and Renee, I'm confused. I'm not even sure I want to continue tithing." I asked Jim how he felt about the fairness of what had happened to them. "Well, it certainly doesn't seem fair on the outside, especially being betrayed by a man I trusted for so many years. But I don't have any problems with God about what happened. I know God is faithful and that he's going to take care of us. Something good will eventually come out of all this."

I wondered if Jim was in some way denying his true feelings, but time has proven that he wasn't. Today, six years later, Jim and Renee are working for a missions organization and living in a nice little condo, and they are as content as they were when they had everything. I talked with Jim recently and sensed that in many ways they are even happier today than they were before. He told me, "We're still committed to not only tithe but to give above and beyond the tithe to people and situations where we can see God at work."

Tom and Jenny, Jim and Renee—two opposing approaches to money and giving.

Some years ago we visited a large church in another area. When it came time for the offering, the pastor asked everyone to get out their offering envelope and to wave it in the air. As he prayed for God to bless the offering, he told God that the waving envelopes were a "wave offering of joy and praise" that represented each person's desire to "give cheerfully." Obviously, over the years, he had been teaching his people the discipline of giving as an act of joy, not an obligation.

Unfortunately, many people see giving as a duty that must be done, and they rebel against that attitude as a form of legalism. Others see giving as a way of getting. They look at the promises in Scripture related to how God blesses those who give, and so they give with the expectation that now God will give back to them. I can remember discussions in Sunday school classes about the tithe—as to whether it was only an Old Testament principle or still applicable to us today. Some of those who felt that it still applied wanted to discuss whether we were supposed to tithe the gross or the net amount from our paychecks. And then there were a few who advanced the argument that since our taxes paid for many things that the tithe used to take care of in the early church, like caring for widows and orphans, shouldn't some part of our taxes be figured into the percentage we give as a tithe?

Each of these concerns clearly misses the real point of the discipline of giving. The ability to give cheerfully arises out of an attitude, and that attitude is the result of the inner discipline of giving simply for the joy of giving. Jim and Renee knew that joy because over the years they had disciplined their hearts to free themselves from being owned by their possessions. The discipline of giving allowed them to very literally say with Paul, "I have learned how to get along happily whether I have much or little. I know how to live on almost nothing or with everything. I have learned the secret of contentment in every situation" (Phil. 4:11-12). That's the end result of giving as a discipline.

But for some people, like us, the joy didn't come first. We just had to make the choice to be obedient and start giving. Some couples say they will start giving "when . . . ," but the "when" never happens, and they never discover the cheerful heart that comes with the discipline of giving.

Giving is seldom included in the lists of disciplines, perhaps because over the centuries, as the disciplines developed, giving was considered a duty that only a few could afford. The disparity between the few who were rich and the masses who were poor led to little being said. Instead, other ways were found to get money for the church. Everything from selling indulgences in the Middle Ages in order to buy one's way out of purgatory to raffles and bake sales helped support the budget.

With the rise of affluence, more attention has been given to giving, but usually not in the context of a spiritual discipline. We give out of guilt, or we give because it is tax deductible. And if we give for these reasons, our giving is going to be sporadic at best or a bone of contention between us at worst.

Along with the rise of affluence has come an increase in debt. Many couples have dug themselves a financial hole. Sometimes the hole is a deep pit that has been there for as long as either one can remember. The desire to give may be there, but the chronic financial problems keep them projecting their ability to give into the future. For others, the struggle to make ends meet is genuine. There is no "pit of debt," only the daily struggle to pay for the basic essentials. How does one give in that context?

Remember, a spiritual discipline within our marriage is an activity that draws us both closer to each other and to God. We are not to give out of a sense of duty, obligation, or debt. Paul tells us that "cheerful givers are the ones God prizes" (2 Cor. 9:7). Seeking giving as a discipline helps us as a couple develop an attitude of "cheerful giving" that comes from the heart. Duty coerces us; discipline is something we choose for reasons that are meaningful to us. If I am living on the edge financially, seeing giving as a discipline that must be developed helps me begin with something small that is an expression of my heart. If God enjoys that attitude within us, then he is certainly going to share with us more of himself as we enter into that process.

✝ MAKING GIVING A VITAL PART
OF LIFE TOGETHER

1. Look at the way you give now. What is your motivation? Are you a cheerful giver? If this is not true for one or both of you, then make changing your attitude your first goal. How can you both become cheerful givers, not only to God, but to other people in your life? What changes do you need to make in your hearts? Base your decision on our description of giving as an activity that can draw us, as a couple, closer to God. Take time as you discuss this decision, and make certain you discuss all the possible wrong motives for wanting to give. Start small, but at least begin to give.

If you are already giving, make a decision together to give more. If you haven't been giving a set amount to the Lord's work, determine to begin to give a certain percentage. Your starting point should stretch your faith and be a demonstration of obedience in this area. As you begin to give this set amount, make it your goal to find ways, over time, to give more. Sometimes when you are just starting to give, it helps to find some project, either within the church or somehow connected to the church, to which you can contribute. Knowing where your money is going can help bring joy into your giving.

When Jan and I really got serious about the discipline of giving, one of the projects we chose involved supporting children in different parts of the world through World Vision. To this day, we have pictures of "our" children on our refrigerator as a reminder of this part of our stewardship. When one of these children graduates from the relief program, we add the picture of a new child. Knowing how that money was being used helped us develop a more cheerful attitude about giving.

Your starting point should stretch your faith and be a demonstration of obedience in this area.

---

2. Together, look at your lifestyle. Are there ways you could simplify your lifestyle so that you could live on less and give more? While you are examining your lifestyle, look at some of the technical aspects related to the managing of your money, such as budgets, retirement plans, and the amount of debt you have.

If this kind of discussion has always brought on an argument, you may be tempted to skip this activity. Jan and I know that experience all too well. We resolved this problem by changing our focus. We found that when our perception was that money was a problem, discussion about money became an even bigger problem. But when we shifted our focus to the discipline of giving cheerfully, that shift in focus gave us a new freedom to discuss money matters that happened to involve giving.

If you still find it difficult to discuss your lifestyle, including budgeting and other related money issues, find a good Christian book on money management and use the discipline of study to find a common ground from which you can discuss these issues. Remember, *control* is at the heart of this issue, but the solution is not for the husband—or the wife—to be in control. The goal is that we allow God to be in control and that both husband and wife are learning to trust him together. The evidence that God is in control is a joyful heart as we give.

3. Bring the discipline of prayer to bear directly on the issue of your money and your giving attitudes. Money is a spiritual issue—Jesus made that clear in Matthew 6:24 when he said that money competes with God for our worship. Since money is a spiritual issue, giving away our money is a spiritual discipline. And it is also an area that the enemy will try to attack and where he will try to keep us in bondage.

Pray together that God will do whatever is necessary for this to become an area of spiritual growth and joy in your marriage. Pray over the specific bills and your deposits, and pray that God will bless your money. It is also important that you pray preventative prayers—that God will protect your finances. And ask God to help you have a joyful spirit as you learn more about the discipline of giving together.

4. Consider ways of giving that are not monetary. Once you have looked at the issues in your marriage involving money, consider ways you can give that are not monetary. One couple we know goes to the Rescue Mission every Thanksgiving and Christmas to help serve the meals. They have family in the area, but the holiday schedule is adjusted so they can give their time to something that is meaningful in their lives. This doesn't take the place of giving financially; it is simply a way to look for other avenues of joyful giving.

HOW GIVING CAN MAKE YOUR
MARRIAGE BETTER

We Discover Who's in Charge
In Tom's mind, either he was in charge or Jenny was, and in the latter case, financial ruin would be the result. To Jim and Renee, God was in charge, so there was no power struggle; that energy was available for better things. They were also freer to give, since they considered money to ultimately belong to God.

Jesus said, "You cannot serve two masters: God and money. For you will hate one and love the other, or else the other way around" (Matt. 6:24). Jesus' next words are, "Don't worry about *things*" (verse 25).

Our worries tell us who or what we are trusting for our security. If I am worried about tomorrow, I am saying that I must somehow control tomorrow, for only then can I let go of my worries. Jesus tells us, "Don't be anxious about tomorrow. God will take care of your tomorrow" (Matt. 6:34). In other words, if I really believe God is in control of tomorrow, I won't worry.

Do we trust God with our tomorrows? The way we handle money is one of the best indicators of our level of trust. We have

*Our worries tell us who or what we are trusting
for our security.*

more freedom to give of our resources if our grip on them is not tight and desperate.

For years, we have been hearing statistics that claim that money management (or the lack of it) is one of the major areas of conflict leading to divorce. That conflict has many roots but is most often a disguised power struggle. Who's going to manage the money and therefore have the power? With this power struggle transformed into a mutual cooperation with God, a couple has defused one of marriage's biggest time bombs.

With this power struggle transformed into a mutual cooperation with God, a couple has defused one of the biggest marriage time bombs.

We Discover Where Our Heart Is

An old fairy tale told by the Brothers Grimm points out that there are two basic approaches to life. Either we are givers or we are takers. In the story "The Fisherman and His Wife,"[1] the man catches a fish that can talk. The fish tells him he is a prince and asks to be let go. The man sets him free.

When the fisherman's wife hears about this amazing fish, she urges him to go back and ask the fish to give them something, like a nice place to live. The man calls the fish, and the fish grants the man's request. When he returns home, his wife is in a beautiful little cottage. Eventually the wife is dissatisfied with the cottage and wants a castle. Then she wants to be queen, then an empress, and then she wants to be the pope. Each of these wishes the enchanted fish grants. Finally, the wife wants to have "the power to make the sun rise!" She asks her husband to ask the special fish to make her "equal to the Creator." The talking fish is fed

1. *A Book of Famous Fairy Tales* (Charles Knapp, 1938), 225–234.

up and tells the man to go home, where he will "find her again in her dirty hovel by the sea!" The Brothers Grimm end the story by saying she was an "example of the consequence of impious ambition." She was a taker whose greedy heart betrayed the fact that she was only interested in getting, not in giving.

In learning to give money, we learn to maintain a general attitude of giving rather than of expecting to be given to and served. Giving cultivates humility. The discipline of giving continually develops in us an awareness of others' needs and thus makes us more ministry oriented. Being in touch with others' neediness can also put a lid on our own self-pity when we don't get all the "things" we think we should have.

We Learn What Is Really Important in Life

Outward appearances would suggest that Tom and Jenny have greater freedom than do Jim and Renee, because Tom and Jenny have more money available to them. While it may be true that they have more freedom of movement, or freedom to *do things,* their money determines that movement. This is not true freedom.

If every time I want to do something, my first and only question is whether or not I have the money, I am not free. When I asked Jim and Renee how they made decisions—both when they had a lot of money and now when they have little—Renee said, "We never let money dictate what we did, and we still don't. Our main concern is what God wants us to do. We've always operated that way." Jim added, "Maybe it was easier when we had money, but we try to see it the same way. If God wants us to do something, he'll provide the way to do it. For us that is genuine freedom!" And they learned this, they said, through faithful giving over the years.

Every time I think of Jim and Renee, I am reminded of what it means to have life in perspective. Our culture worships wealth and sees it as a means to power. But in a marriage, such a struggle

*If every time I want to do something, my first and
only question is whether or not I have
the money, I am not free.*

for power and a grasping after money can only deplete our resources. This doesn't mean we become nonchalant with whatever
material goods God has entrusted to us. Good stewardship
means we are careful, because we are really managing Someone
Else's property.

Several years ago I was in Cambodia teaching basic counseling
skills to a group of young pastors-in-training. They were
students at the Phnom Penh Bible School. While I was there, I
was overwhelmed by the poverty of the people living in that city.
I had my first taste of real culture shock. But I was also amazed at
how these people maintained their dignity, not only in the face of
the poverty, but also in light of the horrible things they had
experienced as a people. My visit to the Killing Fields highlighted
only a small part of the horrors experienced by these people under Pol Pot, a man who could easily be Hitler's equal.

During the week these Bible students were in classes, and on
the weekends they were ministering as pastors throughout the
city and in the villages around the city. They told me about the
church they had started in a nearby village, where approximately
four hundred people had made the decision to become Christians. When they asked if I wanted to visit that village, I eagerly
said yes.

The drive took us along a river where people lived as they had
for centuries. We were blocked on a bridge by people who had
lost legs or arms from the mines planted by Pol Pot and the
Khmer Rouge. We had to give them money in order to cross the
bridge. When we arrived at the village, our interpreter intro-

duced us to some of the elders of the church and their families. And then, together, they proudly took us to the new church they had built. The church was the most beautiful building in the area. Everyone in the village had given so that they could have a church building. No one had coerced them; they gave joyfully out of their money and out of their labor. They gave because they loved Jesus and wanted his house to be the most beautiful one in the village. Even as young believers, they had the right perspective about their lives. They also possessed a joy that transcended the circumstances in which they lived. I want that joy in my life and in my marriage. And the discipline of giving is directly related to the presence of that joy.

TO TALK ABOUT TOGETHER

- Who controls the money in your household? Do you agree with your spouse's answer to that question? If you were to develop ways to share more in the control of the finances, what are some of the problems you might face?
- What are some of your attitudes about giving? Think of times when you gave cheerfully. Think of times when you gave grudgingly or out of duty.
- What areas of your lifestyle are you willing to change? Identify them and then discuss why you are interested in making changes.

THIRTEEN

Silence and Solitude:
A Place to Meet God and Ourselves

IN the course of a discussion on silence and solitude, the question was posed: "How can someone be silent and alone and yet be with their spouse?"

One man answered, "That's easy. Every time my wife and I have an argument, I experience silence and solitude for at least two or three days."

Obviously, not all silences are alike.

For instance, whenever Jan and I take a vacation to one of our favorite places, we experience a certain kind of silence. Each time we have been there, we have followed the same routine: We lie around and read, sleep a lot, eat, and are generally silent. Our silence is largely due to exhaustion, which has been our condition each time we've gone to this particular place. Our emotional and physical state has made it natural for us to begin our vacation time with silence and solitude. Unlike the type of silence experienced by the man noted earlier, ours is mutual, it is a result of our general fatigue, and its purpose is physical and emotional restoration. The silence and solitude the man referred to was imposed by one person, and its purpose was to express anger.

Neither of these silences qualifies as the discipline of silence. This spiritual discipline is mutual, but its purpose is to bring us into a closer relationship to God. Intentionally drawing near to God is what makes an exercise of silence spiritually significant.

Jan and I were talking recently with the couples in our Bible study about our intention to spend several days together in order to experience the spiritual discipline of solitude and silence. We were going to have a silent retreat. After joking together a bit about some of their similar experiences in being silent with each other, we tried to explain the difference between silence out of anger or out of exhaustion and silence and solitude with a specific spiritual purpose. Finally we said, "Wait until we do it, and then we'll tell you the difference."

We made reservations at a retreat center near us that is on the edge of the high desert at the foot of the mountains. It was high enough that the heat wouldn't be overbearing and desolate enough to offer a genuine spiritual retreat. We both said we were looking forward to this experience, but I noticed during the week preceding our trip that I was beginning to pay closer attention to all the unfinished things that needed attention. I didn't say anything, so it surprised me when Jan said she wasn't sure we could afford the time away. We were both a bit apprehensive about this type of silence. But finally one of us said, "No, we're really going to do this."

WHY SILENCE AND SOLITUDE?

A lot is said in the secular culture these days about silence and solitude. To listen to people talk about it, it would be easy to assume that silent retreats began with a monk of some Far Eastern religion. It feels a bit New Age-ish to us. How do silence and solitude apply to Christianity? Are they really necessary and important, or are we just following a cultural craze?

Let's begin by looking at Jesus. He began his ministry only after he had spent forty days alone in the desert (see Matt. 4:1-11). Before making two of his most important decisions, Jesus spent time alone. He did this before choosing the twelve disciples (Luke 6:12), and he did it as he faced the cross (Matt. 26:36-46). Jesus also spent time alone before or after significant events in his life. These include the feeding of the five thousand, the healing of a leper, and the Transfiguration. He personally demonstrated for us the value of solitude and silence—of time alone with God. Silence and solitude in the Christian tradition is a time of being filled up by God, rather than of emptying ourselves of every thought and feeling.

The psalmist urges us several times toward silence and solitude. He writes, "Stand before the Lord in awe, and do not sin against him. Lie quietly upon your bed in silent meditation" (Ps. 4:4). Again he urges us to "stand silent! Know that I am God" (Ps. 46:10). The words of the prophet Isaiah pick up the same refrain when he says, "In quietness and confidence is your strength" (Isa. 30:15). Elijah kept looking for God in the big things, and found him in the gentle breeze, in the sound of silence (1 Kings 19:10-13).

One of the great classics of Christian devotional literature is Thomas à Kempis's book, *Of the Imitation of Christ*. In it, he has a chapter entitled "Of the Love of Solitude and Silence." He begins the chapter by saying:

> Seek a convenient time to retire into thyself, and meditate often upon God's loving-kindnesses. Forsake curious questionings; but read diligently matters which rather yield contrition to thy heart, than occupation to thy head.[1]

1. Thomas à Kempis, *Of the Imitation of Christ* (Oxford University Press, 1900).

He refers to Ecclesiastes 3:1, which says "There is a right time for everything," including "a time to be quiet; a time to speak up" (verse 7). But that quiet time won't happen all by itself; it requires an effort and some planning on our part.

Another woman, when she heard what we were doing, said to Jan, "My husband would love to have a silent retreat. He never leaves the house except to go to work, so he loves solitude. And when he is home, he hardly ever talks. I know he must love silence as well. I guess his whole life is a silent retreat." Her husband's silence was different from the discipline of silence in that his solitude led to emptiness and his silence led to isolation.

Henri Nouwen tells the story of Anthony, a young man who spent many years in solitude. Anthony survived only because of his dependence on the lordship of Jesus Christ, and when he left his solitude, people were drawn to him because he possessed "the qualities of an authentic 'healthy' man, whole in body, mind, and soul." [2] Nouwen points out that whenever we enter into true solitude, we will become aware "of the call to let our false, compulsive self be transformed into the new self of Jesus Christ." [3] Perhaps in some way we already know this—and this is precisely why we avoid being alone.

One can be a hermit in the desert, however, and never experience this kind of solitude. The hermit seeks isolation, whereas the spiritual search for solitude always leads us through anxiety and struggle, but ends with fulfillment. The disciplines of solitude and silence don't simply take us to a place of privacy or retreat from the pressures of life; nor is true solitude merely a place to be physically and emotionally recharged. Jan and I may walk the beach together and feel restored physically and emotionally, but even that is not the same as the spiritual exercise of solitude and silence. When it is a spiritual exercise, I come to that quiet place

2. Henri J. M. Nouwen, *The Way of the Heart* (New York: Ballantine Books, 1981), 7.
3. Ibid., 8.

to meet the Lord, and then to meet myself. In that encounter with Jesus and with myself, solitude and silence can become a place of transformation.

In that encounter with Jesus and with myself, solitude and silence can become a place of transformation.

WHY SOLITUDE AND SILENCE ARE SO DIFFICULT

If the end result of this discipline is to become more like Jesus and to experience more of him in our marriage, why do we resist so much?

Cracking Open Our Shell of Superficial Securities

Every writer who describes the spiritual search for solitude and silence talks about the inner confrontation that will take place. They use words like "furnace," "nothingness," and "death," to describe the experience, and they all point out the great need for the presence of Christ to be with us in the midst of our process. Nouwen noted that brother Anthony needed to cling to Christ in order to survive his solitude. Dallas Willard notes the importance of our "clinging to Christ," because, as he points out, the discipline of solitude and silence "cracks open and bursts apart the shell of our superficial securities."[4]

Even the psalmist notes:

> *I'll keep quiet, especially when the ungodly are around me. But as I stood there silently the turmoil within me grew to the bursting point. The more I mused, the hotter the fires inside. Then at last I spoke and pled with God: Lord, help me to realize how brief my time on earth will be. Help me to know that I am here for but a moment more. My life is no longer than my*

4. Dallas Willard, *The Spirit of the Disciplines* (San Francisco: Harper, 1988), 140.

hand! My whole lifetime is but a moment to you. Proud man! Frail as breath! A shadow! . . . And so, Lord, my only hope is in you. Psalm 39:1-7

The silence brought David to the place of clinging to his hope in God.

Beyond Being a Better Person

Our retreat director told us that other religions use this activity of solitude and silence to calm the mind and to look inward in an attempt to become a better person. "The difference," he said, "between what they do and what we do, is that we go into the silence first to encounter God and then to encounter ourselves. It's a time of intense prayer." And when we bring our superficialities and defenses before God, we encounter his love and acceptance of us in deeper and more powerful ways than ever before.

I talked with a friend who has gone on a silent retreat at least once every three months for a number of years. He related that at first he became very anxious; it seemed that the silence would swallow him up. He wanted to run back to his busy schedule. But he decided instead to look more closely at what this anxiety meant in his life at that moment. What was so terrifying to him? For one thing, he discovered that he does not like being alone with himself. In the silence and solitude, he encounters parts of himself that he does not like.

My friend went on to describe his "cracking open." For him, this meant the shedding of all those things he thought he needed in order to survive—his perceptions of himself, his achievements, and his ability to perform various tasks. But over time he has gradually let go of these supports and defenses, and he is learning to lean more on the reality of Jesus Christ as his source of inner security. What this leads to is a growing ability to accept and even like himself.

When we are faced with seeing the parts of ourselves we have worked so hard to hide, the natural response is to run to our friends, to our busyness, to our work, or to the noise and the clatter of life. But when we persevere in seeking the Lord in solitude and in silence, there is no hiding. And there is a wonderful grace and acceptance we can experience only when we come out of that hiding place.

When faced with seeing difficult things, our natural response is to run to our friends, busyness, work, or the noise and clatter of life.

Solitude and Silence Make a Way for Intimacy

If this is true of the individual who seeks solitude and silence, it is even more true of the couple who together seek spiritual intimacy in this way. There is the added fear that what we are seeing in ourselves will also be seen by our spouse. And our tactics for hiding—which we've spent a lifetime perfecting—will be undone.

What we begin to realize is that the more we become aware of the loving presence of the Lord, the more our fears about being known by our spouse subside. Our purpose in silence and solitude is to meet Jesus. And when we kneel together at his feet, our need to hide begins to dissipate, and our intimacy with God and with each other grows stronger. All of this takes time and experience. Unfortunately, for all too many of us it is much easier to simply avoid these experiences—avoid all that anxiety—forgetting that we will also miss out on the spiritual intimacy we can share and develop.

WHAT ACTUALLY HAPPENED IN OUR RETREAT

When Jan and I finally arrived at our silent retreat, we were ready. We had brought no reading materials other than the Bible.

There were no radios or TVs at the retreat center, and the closest newspaper was fifteen miles away. We asked to meet with one of the retreat leaders and had a wonderful experience talking with him about what we were to do. He said there were other guests there also, but that they would respect our silence. And then he warned us about what to expect.

"This will be difficult. As your mind calms down and you are able to hear the voice of God within you, don't be surprised if you find that God is showing you things about yourself that are painful. You may even feel overwhelmed and unable to sleep," he added, directing us to read Psalm 91 before going to bed. "Ask God to help you sleep and to give your body and mind rest during the night."

We had arrived late in the afternoon, and after settling in it was almost time for dinner. We took some time to work out our schedule since we couldn't talk about it once the silence began. We decided to begin the silence with dinner. The meal was simple, and we ate in silence as someone did some spiritual readings. We listened but did not talk. We noticed that no one at our table made eye contact with us, for they had been told we were on a silent retreat. After dinner we walked awhile in silence and then separately started the process of reading and meditating on John's Gospel.

The next morning as we prepared for breakfast, it seemed awkward not to speak to each other. But we were committed to the silence. As soon as we finished breakfast, each of us went to a different quiet corner of a garden that had been carved out of the desert. At first, my mind raced with all kinds of thoughts. I thought about things I needed to be doing, letters I hadn't written, and phone calls I should have been making. I tried to focus on the readings but missed the background music that usually helps me concentrate. After a while, I noted that I felt like a restless kid in church—I could hardly sit still. Jan reported later that she had had similar difficulties. But we stayed with our silence.

After about two and a half hours alone in the garden, we headed back to our room to relax, still keeping the silence. The retreat leader had told us that we would probably be drained by our silence. He suggested we read something for fun. Since we hadn't brought anything but our Bibles, I read Esther and Jan skimmed some of the Psalms. He even suggested we take a nap after lunch, which we did. Then we went to our separate parts of the garden for another session with the Lord. The plan we followed for each of the two-and-a-half-hour sessions with God was to first spend some time reading John's Gospel. We were to read slowly until something stopped us—a word or phrase that caught our attention—and then we were to meditate on that particular verse or phrase. I found that my time in John's Gospel took about forty-five minutes. Then, in an effort to calm my thoughts, I simply meditated on Jesus' name. I found that, for me, the second period of silence and prayer was very different from what I had experienced that morning. I was able to quiet my spirit, and God did bring something specific about me to my attention. I spent over an hour in silent prayer, talking with God about one particular aspect of me that was not very desirable or pleasant. I had never spent that much time so intensely in prayer before. I could hardly believe the time when I finally checked my watch.

Jan still struggled with the second session. Gradually, though, by next morning's session, her mind started to slow down and she experienced the same type of time with the Lord as I had had the previous afternoon. That evening, the retreat director suggested that we go to the chapel and spend some time in intense intercessory prayer. He suggested we use Colossians 4:12 as the basis of our praying. Paul wrote that "Epaphras . . . is always earnestly praying for you, asking God to make you strong and perfect and to help you know his will in everything you do." One translation says that Epaphras "is always wrestling in prayer for you" (NIV). The retreat director suggested we pray with fervor and wrestle for the souls of those we were praying for.

When it came time to break our silence, I think we were both surprised by the sense of oneness we had experienced with each other. We had expected to experience a closeness and intimacy with God, but wondered what effect the silence would have on us.

When it came time to break our silence, I think we were both surprised by the sense of oneness we had experienced with each other.

At first, we said the things we had struggled *not* to say during the silence (although Jan slipped and said a few words a couple of times, and I slipped and said half of a sentence once). We talked about the ducks at the lake that Jan fed after each meal. We talked about the beauty of the garden, which we learned had been all desert only thirty years earlier. Now it was surrounded by trees soaring forty to fifty feet into the air.

We were almost reluctant to return home, because the warmth of our silent retreat was so refreshing. We were physically drained by the time in silence but were very alert emotionally. For several days afterward, we talked about things we had learned about ourselves, about God, and about our busyness. We determined that times away in silence were to be a part of our life together from then on.

MAKING SILENCE AND SOLITUDE A VITAL PART OF LIFE TOGETHER

Begin slowly. This is especially important if you have never been on a silent retreat, or if this spiritual discipline is completely new to you. You might begin by talking together about the meaning of Ecclesiastes 3:7. How does "a time to be quiet; a time to speak up" relate to you and your marriage? Spend some time talking about the meaning of silence in your experience, and listen to your partner tell about his or her feelings. Talk about the idea of setting aside specific times for silence together.

If you find that only one of you is interested in making silence and solitude a part of your marriage, slow down even more. Review what we said earlier about how to respond to your partner's resistance to any of these disciplines. If it is important to you but not to your mate, you especially need to slow down, for pressure will only increase resistance.

Start big. Jan and I felt that we needed a retreat that would clearly be a break from our routine. We planned a two-day silent retreat at a retreat center during the week. We chose a retreat center because we did not want to have to think about meals, and because retreat centers are often set off by themselves in a natural setting, which fosters a sense of solitude.

Look for a place near you where you can get away. Then plan your time together. We were silent for the whole time, but set our times of solitude to be from 8:30 A.M. to 11:00 A.M. and from 3:30 P.M. to 6:00 P.M.. We napped after lunch and then spent about an hour after dinner in intercessory prayer in the chapel. All we took to the retreat center, besides clothes, etc., were Bibles and notebooks. Some people bring inspirational reading materials. Our retreat director even suggested bringing some light, entertaining reading to provide a brief change of pace during the middle of the day.

The purpose of the silence is twofold. First, it helps calm your mind so that you can hear your heart. And second, it helps you focus more on what God wants you to hear and understand about him and about yourself, your relationship with him, and your relationship with your spouse.

Focus on God's Word. As you approach the periods of solitude and silence, first spend some time reading through a predetermined passage of Scripture. We started reading John's Gospel. Read slowly and reverently until something strikes you, then stop and meditate on what that passage is saying to you. After you meditate on the passage, pray that passage for yourself.

For example, I was struck by John 4:50: "The man took Jesus at his word and departed" (NIV). I spent time meditating on what it means to me to take Jesus at his word. I asked myself why I was struck by that phrase. What did it mean to me? Then I spent time praying about different areas of my life in which I don't take Jesus at his word, asking him to help me understand the barriers within me. After praying the passage, I simply sat silently for a while, allowing myself to assimilate what I had just experienced. That took about an hour. Then I sat silently and focused my mind on Jesus for a while. I asked him to show me what I needed to face within myself and for him to help me look at whatever he brought to my mind.

Finally, I spent some time writing in my journal what God had been showing me, both within the Scripture and within my time of silence. The rest of the time we both spent reading different parts of the Scripture and also simply rested and prayed. That's how we did it. There are other ways to enjoy silence and solitude spiritually, so don't be afraid to vary the procedures to fit your personalities and styles.

Create a "quiet place" at home. One of the things I noted during one period of reflection was that I wanted to work on creating a garden area in our yard where we could have a "quiet place" at home. You may want to create such a place to be together with the Lord around your home, either inside or outside. Some choose to have two special chairs set in a comfortable place together, and the family knows that when they are in those chairs, they are in a place of quiet and solitude.

Others we know have created a special place of prayer in their home. One friend found an antique kneeling bench and set it up within their den. When they want to have their quiet place, they go and kneel on that old kneeling bench. Sometimes they do this alone; other times they go together to that place. Having a familiar place that you can use often will help when it comes to quieting your mind.

Having a familiar place that you can use often will help when it comes to quieting your mind.

When we talk about having a place of silence that only one of you can use at a time, the intimacy together comes later as you share what you experienced in your time of silence and solitude. Always follow your times of silence and solitude with a time for reflective sharing together.

Find the quiet places that are already present. Even before we create a garden place, we can find places of quiet and solitude if we look for them. We noted earlier that the psalmist said, "Lie quietly upon your bed in silent meditation" (Ps. 4:4). We all have times of sleeplessness in the night—and we can use such times for silent meditation.

Perhaps you like to have your morning coffee early. Why not go off to your quiet corner together and enjoy a time of silence for a while? Leave the newspaper for later, and use that time of quiet reflection to meditate upon the Lord. If you have a long commute to work, turn off the radio and use the time of silence and solitude (which *can* take place in the midst of hurry and crowdedness), and talk to God.

Agree upon a certain space of silence during a specific day. You might set aside a period of four hours during which you will be silent. You may take that time to read and meditate on a specific passage of Scripture or a devotional passage from some other book or magazine. It is important when you set these times that you also agree on their focus. Without a focus, it will be too easy to let your mind wander or simply take a much-needed nap.

Come together at the end of silence and solitude. Paul Stevens quotes Henri Nouwen's statement that "without solitude there can be no real people"[4] and adds the thought that "without shared solitude, there can be no real marriage." The real joy of shared solitude and silence is the coming together when it ends and the time of sharing with each other what you have discovered about yourself and about God. Don't miss that special part of the spiritual discipline of solitude and silence.

HOW SILENCE AND SOLITUDE CAN MAKE YOUR MARRIAGE BETTER

We've noted that one of the benefits of the spiritual discipline of solitude and silence is the ability to come out of hiding and be free to become more of who we really are. Another benefit is that as we encounter our own sinfulness, there is also a growing compassion within us for others. The more honestly I see myself before God, the more the distance between myself and others shrinks. The truth of the fact that we are all sinners becomes clearer to me, and as I experience God's grace toward me in my own sinfulness, I can also begin to experience greater compassion toward others.

The other benefit is related to the tongue. James has a lot to say about the power the tongue has over our lives. He says, "If anyone can control his tongue, it proves that he has perfect control over himself in every other way. . . . So also the tongue is a small thing, but what enormous damage it can do" (James 3:2,

4. Paul Stevens, *Marriage Spirituality* (Downers Grove, Ill.: InterVarsity Press, 1989), 70.

5). He goes on to add that "no human being can tame the tongue. It is always ready to pour out its deadly poison" (verse 8).

When we observe periods of silence, we are exercising control over our tongue for that period of time. I found it very difficult to stop talking, especially in the beginning. There were so many good things I wanted to say. But I had chosen silence, and so for two days, I "tamed my tongue." In doing so I experienced a degree of self-control that allowed me to hear the still, small voice of God.

In taming my tongue, I experienced a degree of self-control that allowed me to hear the voice of God.

TO TALK ABOUT TOGETHER

- In what ways have you used silence in your marriage? Discuss how it can be used constructively and how it can be used destructively.
- In what ways have you avoided silence in your life? What do you think you would encounter in silence?
- Where are some "quiet places" you could develop around your home? What first steps can you take to create those places?
- What kind of retreat resources are in your area? Conduct some research, and talk together about special places you might go to or retreat services you could utilize together.

FOURTEEN

The Lord's Fast:
It's More Than Going Hungry

EARLIER this year, our local newspaper did a feature article describing the Islamic holy month of Ramadan. For thirty days, Muslims all over the world abstain from all food and liquids during the daylight hours. In some Muslim countries the Ramadan fast is obligatory. But here in southern California the fast is done voluntarily.

As I read the article, in which several Muslims were interviewed about the meaning of their fasting, I was struck by the strong spiritual motivation each of them had to participate in the fast. They made it clear that in some families not everyone participated, but for those who did, it was clear that the fast was an integral part of their worship. Each one interviewed commented on how the daily fast caused discomfort, especially at the beginning, but that it increased their hunger for God.

I was convicted in my own spirit as I read about their fast. They get up early in the morning, while it is still dark, to have breakfast and spend time in prayer. Then they abstain from food, liquids, medicine, and sexual relations until after sunset. It is a very difficult form of fasting in that they abstain from drinking any form of liquid throughout the day, which can cause some degree of dehydration and additional discomfort.

Jan and I have fasted at various times over the years. Sometimes we fasted for a day in order to diet. Other times our fasting has been limited to a particular meal on one day, when instead of eating, we spend the time praying in agreement for some specific situation. As I read the newspaper article, I felt rather lazy in my approach to this particular spiritual activity.

I don't remember hearing anything about fasting while I was growing up. I don't remember hearing my parents talk about it, and I can't remember hearing any sermons on the subject. Richard Foster notes that between the years of 1861 and 1954, not one book was published on the subject of fasting.[1] I guess my growing-up years were part of that period when fasting was ignored. On the other hand, Jan says she heard about fasting while she was growing up, because several of the older saints in her church would talk about "fasting and praying." But no one talked about it from the pulpit or in Sunday school classes.

What is surprising about those years of silence on the subject of fasting is that the Bible is not at all silent about it. When you look at who fasted in the Bible, the list is too long to detail. Moses fasted for forty days and nights, without food or water. All the Jews were to fast on the Day of Atonement. David fasted for seven days when his child by Bathsheba was dying. Several times Jeremiah and Daniel fasted. Esther asked her people to fast for three days and nights, abstaining from both food and liquids. She followed the fast along with all the Jews in her town. Jesus fasted for forty days in the wilderness. Paul fasted for three days after his encounter with Jesus on the Damascus road. The early Chris-

1. Richard Foster, *The Celebration of Discipline* (San Francisco: Harper & Row, 1988), 47.

tians are described in Acts as "fasting and praying" together. It was clearly something done regularly by those who sought to know God, in both the Old and New Testaments. In all, the Bible contains nearly sixty references to fasting.

Why did fasting become the forgotten discipline? Perhaps because some made fasting a rule, rather than a choice, thereby creating the opportunity for abuse. The abuse of fasting is seen early on in the Gospels when Jesus made note of the Pharisees' habit of fasting twice a week. He pointed out that they fasted in order to impress others by trying "to look wan and disheveled so people will feel sorry for them" (Matt. 6:16). The fast days of the Pharisees were also the public market days, making it easy for others to observe their "holiness."

Other Christian leaders have been so profoundly affected by the benefits of fasting that they sought to make it a rule for all Christians. During the Middle Ages, fasting often became an obsession. Monks lived only on bread and water. One devout seeker ate no cooked food for seven years. Even John Wesley "refused to ordain anyone to the Methodist ministry who did not fast" on Wednesdays and Fridays.[2] Perhaps the abuses of not only fasting but of many of the spiritual disciplines led to their being ignored by many Christians, who saw them only as part of a "works-oriented" approach to faith. Unfortunately, the rich spiritual experiences available to us through these disciplines were also lost.

The Scriptures never present fasting as an obligation for Christians. We don't "have to" fast. But it seems to be assumed that Christians will fast. Jesus started his teaching about fasting in Matthew 6:16 with the words, "When you fast . . . ," not "If you fast" or "You must fast." Fasting, like giving, is not an obligation (2 Cor. 9:7). It is a choice.

2. Ibid., 51.

WHAT MAKES A FAST SPIRITUAL?

The dictionary first defines a fast as "to abstain from all food." The second definition is "to eat only sparingly or of certain kinds of food, esp. as a religious observance."[3] Both are considered a "fast." For example, our doctor may tell us to "fast" before our physical examination, meaning that we are not to eat or drink anything between going to bed and visiting his office the next day. Or a diet center may suggest that we "fast" one day a week as a means to lose weight or to maintain our weight loss. Both of these are fasts, but neither is a spiritual exercise.

It might help us better understand the difference if we call a "fast" a "diet" when its purpose is to lose weight. And when the purpose of our "diet" is for our spiritual welfare, then we call it a "fast." Can we do both at the same time? Of course. In fact, whenever we diet, we would be wise to seek the spiritual benefits as well as the physical. But fasting is a spiritual discipline only when we are seeking some spiritual growth or enrichment in the process. In fact, usually a fast is seen as spiritual when it is coupled with prayer; in the Scriptures as well as in present-day practice, we see that fasting and praying usually go together.

✝ MAKING FASTING A VITAL PART OF LIFE TOGETHER

1. Begin small. Like any form of exercise, you don't tackle the big things until you are comfortable with the smaller things. I would suggest you begin by fasting for one meal. Several years ago, Jan and I agreed with several other couples that we would fast and pray for one meal each week over a period of six months, taking that time to fast and pray about some very specific need in the lives of one of the couples. It was a very powerful experience, not

3. *Webster's College Dictionary* (New York: Random House, 1991).

only because we saw God work in the lives of that couple, but also because God did a work in our own lives as well.

Often, in the course of our conversation, Jan or I will suggest that we fast during a particular mealtime and pray over a concern we've been discussing. There is real value in fasting over a period of time, so you might want to pick one meal a week for six months and agree to fast and pray during that time. Since you are doing this as a couple, it is always important to talk together about your experiences.

Even if you are only going to fast for one meal, it is important

---

Jan or I will suggest that we fast during a particular mealtime and pray over a concern we've been discussing.

---

that you drink a lot of water during that time and that if there are any medical conditions that might be affected by your fasting, you check with your physician first.

2. Move on to longer fasts. Once you are comfortable with missing a meal, try a twenty-four-hour or thirty-six-hour fast. When you do a twenty-four-hour fast, you really only miss two meals. For example, if you go from noon one day to noon the next day, you will miss dinner and breakfast. A thirty-six-hour fast will usually begin when you go to bed one night and finish when you get up two days later. Basically, you will fast for an entire day. Whenever you feel hungry, drink plenty of water. The hunger you do feel will only be the result of your stomach preparing for the meals it usually receives at those particular times. Again, use the time when you would normally eat for prayer, meditation, and worship.

3. Make it a regular exercise. After you have successfully experienced several different time periods of fasting, along with a sense of spiritual awareness, talk together about establishing a regular program of fasting. Commit to a regular practice of fasting together as part of your spiritual worship.

HOW FASTING CAN MAKE
YOUR MARRIAGE BETTER

It Helps Us Follow the Examples of Spiritual People before Us
Perhaps the best reason we fast is to follow the examples of those we meet in the Scriptures. If Moses, David, Ezra, Esther, Mordecai, Jeremiah, Daniel, Joel, Zechariah, Anna, Jesus, Paul, and Barnabas all practiced fasting, then there must be spiritual value in this discipline. One reason these people fasted was to more clearly focus their attention on God and to worship and fellowship with him. For Jesus, fasting was a part of the way he centered himself in his heavenly Father's will.

We read that the prophetess Anna worshiped God "by praying and often fasting" (Luke 2:36-37). Fasting and prayer were a part of her worship. This means that fasting is an attitude of the heart that seeks to control our physical appetites. As we experience physical hunger, we can direct that hunger toward God. We see this in the experience of the church at Antioch. We read that when Paul and Barnabas, and several other men, "were worshiping and fasting the Holy Spirit said, 'Dedicate Barnabas and Paul for a special job I have for them.' So after more fasting and prayer, the men laid their hands on them—and sent them on their way" (Acts 13:2-3). Here worshiping and fasting are closely intertwined.

It Helps Us Develop a Greater Sense of Intimacy with One Another
Whenever Jan and I fast together, even if I am at the office and she is at home, we find that our sense of togetherness in this discipline increases our sense of oneness. There is something powerful in two people, who may even be separated by distance,

agreeing to block out a mealtime in order to focus on some spiritual issue together with the Lord. As we meet God individually, there seems to be a spiritual dynamic that is at work also. In our coming together before the Lord for the same purpose, our hearts are knit together in his presence. And when we are together physically in the same room and share our individual experience of our fast, that shared intimacy with the Lord is enlarged even more.

---

*There is something powerful in two people agreeing
to block out a mealtime in order to focus on
some issue together with the Lord.*

It Helps Us Shore Up Our Strength and Wisdom during Challenging Times

Throughout history, those who were in Christian leadership fasted, especially in times of challenge. The example of Esther helps us see this as a reason for us to fast. Haman, the prime minister and the second most powerful man in the Babylonian government, was very angry at Mordecai, the uncle of Esther. Because of his anger at Mordecai, he plotted to have all the Jews killed on a specific day some months later. Esther was queen of the land, but it was not known that she was a Jew. When the edict was published throughout the kingdom, all the Jews mourned, fasted, and wept in despair at the king's decree.

Esther knew nothing of the plot until Mordecai came to the gate of the palace in sackcloth and ashes. When Mordecai sent word back to Esther of Haman's plot to kill all the Jews, he reminded Esther that she would lose her life as well. Esther's response was immediate. She sent word to Mordecai to "go and gather together all the Jews of Shushan and fast for me; do not eat or drink for three days, night or day; and I and my maids will do the same; and then, though it is strictly forbidden, I will go in to see the king; and if I perish, I perish" (Esther 4:16). In a time of crisis, both in the Bible and throughout church history, leaders and followers alike are called to "fast and pray."

Joel calls upon the people to repent from their sin in order to avoid the impending judgment of God. He urges the priests to "announce a fast; call a solemn meeting. Gather the elders and all the people into the Temple of the Lord your God, and weep before him there" (Joel 1:14). He repeats this call again later, saying "Sound the trumpet in Zion! Call a fast and gather all the people together for a solemn meeting" (Joel 2:15).

After Jonah went through the city of Nineveh preaching judgment, the king of Nineveh "sent this message throughout the city: 'Let no one, not even the animals, eat anything at all, nor even drink any water. Everyone must wear sackcloth and cry mightily to God, and let everyone turn from his evil ways, from his violence and robbing" (Jon. 3:7-8).

Daniel was taken captive to Babylon. One of the first things he did there was a type of fasting—he abstained from the food and wine given to him by the king, asking instead to be able to eat as a Jew (see Daniel 1:12). Apparently at a later time, Daniel received a vision. "When this vision came to me [Daniel said later], I had been in mourning for three full weeks. All that time I tasted neither wine nor meat, and, of course, I went without desserts. I neither washed nor shaved nor combed my hair" (10:3).

When Jehoshaphat was King of Judah, three different armies declared war upon them. "Jehoshaphat was badly shaken by this news and determined to beg for help from the Lord; so he announced that all the people of Judah should go without food for a time, in penitence and intercession before God" (2 Chron. 20:3). Again, in times of crisis, God's people have often been called upon to fast and pray.

I think it is important to note that in each of these situations, the purpose of fasting was not to get God to do something someone wanted. It was not a way to bribe God to act. Our attitude in fasting and praying is to be like the attitude of the king of Nineveh, who said, "Who can tell? Perhaps even yet God will decide to let us live and will hold back his fierce anger from destroying us" (Jon. 3:9). We present our need, our crisis, to the Lord, and then allow fasting to subdue our own natural appetites and stir up within us a greater appetite for God, regardless of the outcome.

We present our need to the Lord . . . and stir up
within us a greater appetite for God,
regardless of the outcome.

It Develops True Humility in Us

David writes, "My zeal for God and his work burns hot within me. And because I advocate your cause, your enemies insult me even as they insult you. How they scoff and mock me when I mourn and fast before the Lord!" (Ps. 69:9-10). Another translation says, "I humbled my soul with fasting" (NRSV).

Richard Foster points out that "more than any other discipline, fasting reveals the things that control us."[4] It's humbling to admit that I am controlled by something like my pride or my anger or rebelliousness. But when I fast and pray, God will clearly show me what controls me. My pride can be seen as similar to the pride of the Pharisees, who wanted others to know about their fasts. My resistance to persevering in my fast may at first be blamed on my being too hungry or on my having some other pressure bearing down on me. But if I persevere, not only in fasting but also in praying, God may help me see a spirit of rebelliousness deeper within that needs to be humbled.

4. Richard Foster, *The Celebration of Discipline* (San Francisco: Harper & Row, 1988), 55.

The even more obvious controlling influence could be food. Most of us are preoccupied with food. Try watching television while you are fasting. You will be overwhelmed by the number of commercials that are food-oriented. And the food they show on the screen makes you overwhelmingly aware of your hunger! The messages about food in our culture are contradictory—we are told that in order to be popular, we must be thin. But we are also told to eat three large meals each day and to have several snacks and desserts in between. No wonder we have an epidemic of eating disorders. It's hard to escape the fact that food controls us in so many ways. Fasting helps us see this control for what it is.

It Puts Us in Touch with Our True Source

Fasting helps us understand what really sustains us in this life. After Jesus talked with the Samaritan woman, his disciples tried to get him to eat. He told them, "'No, . . . I have some food you don't know about.' 'Who brought it to him?' the disciples asked each other. Then Jesus explained: 'My nourishment comes from doing the will of God who sent me, and from finishing his work'" (John 4:32-34). Fasting reminds us of this heavenly nourishment.

When Satan tempted Jesus following his forty-day fast in the wilderness by suggesting that Jesus turn stones into bread, Jesus told him, "No! For the Scriptures tell us that bread won't feed men's souls: obedience to every word of God is what we need" (Matt. 4:4). In fasting, we are abstaining from food, but at the same time we are to be "feasting" on the words of God and doing his will. That's why Jesus tells us to avoid being sad when we fast. "When you fast, put on festive clothing, so that no one will suspect you are hungry, except your Father who knows every secret. And he will reward you" (Matt. 6:17-18). Be festive, he says. It is a time of joy, for it represents your freedom from your appetites!

By experiencing freedom from our appetites, fasting also helps us keep balance in our lives. One cannot fast forever, for that would become starvation. But the cycle between fasting and normal eating provides us with an experience of balance between the values of this earthly life and the values of our spiritual life in Christ.

By experiencing freedom from our appetites, fasting also helps us keep balance in our lives.

It Helps Us Attune Ourselves to God

When Jehoshaphat called the people together to fast and pray, a vast army was coming against them. He asked the people to give themselves over to the will of God as he prayed, "O our God, won't you stop them? We have no way to protect ourselves against this mighty army. We don't know what to do, but we are looking to you" (2 Chron. 20:12).

God heard their prayers and answered, "You will not need to fight! Take your places; stand quietly and see the incredible rescue operation God will perform for you, O people of Judah and Jerusalem! Don't be afraid or discouraged! Go out there tomorrow, for the Lord is with you!" (verse 17). Through fasting and prayer, they aligned themselves with the Lord Almighty. We can do the same and join in the work God is already doing.

TO TALK ABOUT TOGETHER

- Talk about what you were taught or what you heard about fasting when you were growing up. Discuss together some of the differences as well as the similarities. Discuss any experiences you have had with fasting.
- Do you remember anyone ever talking about "fasting

and praying"? Do you know anyone who fasts? Why do you think fasting has been such a neglected teaching?

- Discuss some of your hesitations about fasting. Which of the six purposes for fasting do you find most encouraging?

FIFTEEN

The Sabbath Rest:
Bringing Some of Heaven to Earth

WHEN I was growing up, Sunday was the worst day of the week. I hated everything about it. Looking back at it now, I realize that it wasn't that awful, but for me as a boy it sure was. The most miserable part of Sunday was that we weren't allowed to get or even read the Sunday paper. That meant I never got to read the Sunday comics. If you ask how that affected me, I could tell you that today the only paper we have delivered to our home is the Sunday paper, and the comics are the first thing I read. Our family didn't get a TV until I was probably in the ninth grade—not because they weren't invented yet, but because my parents weren't that certain that TV wasn't the devil's invention. So obviously, we did not watch TV on Sunday, but I was allowed to listen to the radio in my room, as long as the volume was low.

I wasn't allowed to go outside and play on Sunday like everyone else in our neighborhood. My friends acted as if they understood; they never came looking for me and soon stopped asking me for reasons. What I *was* allowed to do was go to Sunday

193

school and church in the morning and to church again in the evening. Sometimes we went out for Sunday dinner, and if the spring weather was especially nice, we went to the art museum and walked around the lake in the park outside. My definition of Sunday as a boy would have been "deadening boredom and humiliation!" My family's approach to Sundays was unique only in our neighborhood—everyone else who went to our church did the same thing.

I think my first major act of rebellion as a young person was to sneak off to a Cleveland Browns football game with the preacher's son on a Sunday afternoon. I don't remember how we got out of church, but I do remember that I didn't really enjoy the game, for I was certain that something dreadful was going to happen to me because I was doing such an unspiritual thing on Sunday.

The neighborhood in which I grew up was primarily Jewish, and many of our Jewish neighbors attended a very conservative synagogue. One Saturday, when I was eight or nine years old, I was walking to the bakery that was several blocks from my house. An older man came out on his porch and asked me if I could help him. I agreed, and he led me through his darkened house to the kitchen. He asked if I could turn off the gas flame on his stove. I must have looked at him quizzically, for as I turned off the flame, he told me that it was his Sabbath, and he wasn't allowed to do any work. He also said that was the reason the house was so dark—he couldn't even turn a light switch on or off. So he got me to turn off the stove for him. I don't know who had turned it *on* for him—perhaps another Gentile kid walking to the store earlier!

My experiences of Sunday, which we called the Sabbath, did very little to prepare my heart to understand the meaning of Sabbath rest. At my house it meant we slept most of Sunday afternoon, for there was little else to do. At that Jewish man's house, it meant that someone else had to turn his stove on and off so he could keep the letter of the law while breaking the spirit of the law. Both approaches would qualify as legalism. Only much later did I recognize that both of those experiences were really miles away from what God intended the Sabbath to be.

My experiences of Sunday did very little to prepare
my heart to understand the meaning
of Sabbath rest.

THE DEFINITION OF SABBATH

Some years ago I was the speaker at a retreat for a denomination that believes worship should still be on Saturday. During one of the breaks, I had a long discussion with one of the older men, who had a warm spirit about our differences. I was surprised to find that he wasn't concerned too much with which day of the week we observed. He was more concerned about what he believed to be a divinely inspired rhythm for life, by which we work six days a week and then have one day on which we don't work. To him, the Sabbath was a principle that said one day a week was to be different from the other six days.

He pointed out to me that in the commandment concerning the Sabbath (as well as in Exod. 23:12), the one-day-in-seven rhythm was also for the animals, and it was also applied in years to the land—the fields, vineyards, and olive groves (verses 10-11). To him, all of creation functioned best when it honored the one-in-seven rhythm. His ideas penetrated even my resistance, which came out of my boyhood experiences. I was intrigued by the idea. After all, keeping the Sabbath is one of the Ten Commandments.

When we go to the dictionary to define Sabbath, Webster is willing to accommodate both perspectives, speaking in the first definition about Saturday and in the second definition about

Sunday. In the third definition, Webster simply says it is "a day of rest or prayer." That definition certainly relates to my childhood experience of prayer in church and afternoon naps at home.

I noticed that, coming after "Sabbath" in the dictionary, was "sabbatical." As a member of the faculty at Fuller's School of Psychology, I am entitled to a sabbatical. Only as I read the word in the dictionary did I connect it with the Sabbath. My sabbatical is one quarter off for every six quarters I teach, or one year off for every six years I teach. Even the academic sabbatical is based on the principle of "one-in-seven."

More Than a Nap

The Jewish theologian Abraham Heschel describes more accurately the meaning of the Sabbath than the Jewish man did for me as a boy. He says, "Judaism is a religion of time aiming at the sanctification of time. . . . The Sabbaths are our great cathedrals, and our Holy of Holies is a shrine that neither the Romans nor the Germans were able to burn."[1] For him, the cathedral created by the Sabbath is a place apart from the rest of the world. It represents the sanctification of time. By this he refers to "the day on which we are called upon to share in what is eternal in time, to turn from the world of creation to the creations of the world."[2]

Heschel says that when we understand this one-in-seven rhythm, we can see that the Sabbath stands in judgment of our one-dimensional lives. Once every seven days we are reminded that there is more to this life than what we see. It draws us back from our preoccupation with things and achievements. One day a week we stop our attempts to conquer nature or the corporation. The Sabbath gives us some degree of independence from our civilization and its materialism and connects us with the eternal.

So how does this one day in seven take us beyond the mun-

1. Abraham Joshua Heschel, *The Sabbath: Its Meaning for Modern Man* (New York: Farrar, Straus, 1948), 216.   2. Ibid., 218.

dane to the eternal? Certainly it is not just by taking naps or avoiding the Sunday paper. What we are to do is create a day that is different from the other six days, and we are to do things that orient us toward God and his gifts to us. In essence, it is a time for "holy play and leisure"—for spiritual, physical, and emotional renewal.

We are to create a day that is different from the other six days, to do things that orient us toward God and his gifts to us.

Family and friends have always been a big part of the traditional Jewish Sabbath. Their Sabbath begins at sundown on Friday evening, and this beginning is marked by a special meal of special foods, along with special clothes. This Sabbath meal is a time when family and guests come together to enjoy what is to be the best meal of the week. It is a time everyone anticipates throughout the week. Then time is spent the next morning at Sabbath services, and the rest of the day is available for all the things we are too busy to do during the rest of the week. It can involve reading a book, walking on the beach, laughing with friends, or writing a letter—all as part of the recognition that God and all of his creation are there for our *enjoyment*. The Sabbath is supposed to be a little bit of heaven here on earth. Creating joy on a Sabbath day is what I missed growing up. According to Heschel, it is to be the crowning glory of the week.

Finding God in His Rest As Well As in His Work

A big part of our observation of the Sabbath is the recognition that God is the Creator of all things. As we take our focus away from the pressures of our everyday lives, we focus instead on our Savior, the one who is "the Creator who made everything in heaven and earth, the things we can see and the things we can't; the spirit world with its kings and kingdoms, its rulers and authorities; all were made by Christ for his own use and glory. He was before all else began and it is his power that holds everything together" (Col. 1:16-17). When we do this, we go beyond legalism and sterility (so well represented by my childhood experiences) and can find the true enjoyment God intended for that day.

The purpose of our spiritual disciplines is to help us together to find intimacy with God not only in his work but also in his rest. In the Jewish tradition, there are a number of negative rules for the Sabbath. They include things that imply "resting" from what we do the rest of the week: We are "not to mourn, not to confess sins, not to repent, not to do anything that might lead to unhappiness." [3] In the Jewish tradition, and even more for believers in Christ, the heart of the Sabbath is to be an experience of differentness, a day of rest and joy, especially spiritual joy.

The Problem with Finding Time
When we talk about setting aside one day in seven, your reaction is probably the same as mine: "I don't have the time!" But that's the point. We must make time. It is only when we discipline ourselves in this way that we can say we are in control of our schedule. This is one day of the week on which time serves us, rather than our schedules ruling us. This is one way in which we sanctify the time that is given to us.

This is one day of the week on which time serves us, rather than our schedules ruling us.

Remember also that the Sabbath is one of the "putting off" disciplines, which means that we will have to let go of some things

3. Jacob Neusner, *The Enchantments of Judaism* (New York: Basic Books, 1987), 95.

in our lives in order to make some adjustments in our activities and priorities. Here, the end justifies the means. Whatever it takes to bring your schedule under control so that you can have the time for a Sabbath rest will bring your heart closer to the priorities God has for your life.

I think another reason people don't practice the "one-in-seven" principle is that it feels as if we are following the law; it feels like the old legalism. We believe that since "our salvation does not depend on keeping the law but on receiving God's grace" (Rom. 6:15), we are free from the law, and keeping the Sabbath is part of that law. That's true! But our discipline of the Sabbath is not done to impress God with our law keeping. We keep the Sabbath because we recognize God's "one-in-seven" principle as a way of life.

 MAKING THE SABBATH A VITAL PART
OF LIFE TOGETHER

Settle your definitions. Take some time to define together your personal understanding of the meaning of "holy play" or "holy leisure." We begin, of course, with corporate worship, where we join together with others in the body of Christ to worship him. But we also want to look beyond the time we spend with other believers at our church. Look for some other definitions you share that go beyond corporate worship, and then choose one thing that you could plan to do together that would be an expression of your definition. Plan to do it together on one of the next few Sundays. You may only be able to begin with one hour on Sunday that you make different (not counting church). But begin with that hour and plan it so that you can experience a little bit of heaven here on earth.

Work on "one-in-seven" with your children. If you have children at home, discuss some ways you can help them understand the "one-in-seven" principle represented by the Sabbath. How can you make this a fun day for them as well? Perhaps it can be a day when you play games together, take special trips together, and plan special events as a family. But keep a balance between what you do as a family and what you do as a couple. Your children will learn the most when they see you enjoy the day together in special ways.

Write about it—then compare notes. Take some time alone and write out what you would like to do together if you had a special day reserved just for the two of you. After you have written it out, share it with your mate. You may find that your "days" are very similar—or perhaps they are very different. Talk together about how you experience a part of your special day on a "Sabbath" day. Set a date and do it.

Build a cathedral. After you have done the first two or three activities, set some time aside to discuss how you could take a day and "build a cathedral" together. By this I mean you plan a day where most of what you do sets you apart spiritually and recreationally from the activity of the rest of your week. For example, one of the things we enjoy about Sunday is having all of our kids and grandchildren over for Sunday dinner following church. They seem to enjoy it, for they often stay around for the whole afternoon. When they are there, we don't do what we might be tempted to do if they weren't there—which would probably be more of what we do the rest of the week.

What we do the rest of the week is precisely what Jan and I are trying to avoid now on our Sabbath. We are working on our list of "don'ts" that will help us make this one-day-in-seven special and enjoyable: I don't write; Jan doesn't take things back to the department store or run other errands. We don't do chores around the house. We aren't setting these up as legalistic rules, but only as reminders of how we can, once a week, build a spiritual cathedral in our lives. As we create a "don't," we also create some time for a special "do" that we've been putting off doing together.

Building a cathedral is something you may want to do with other couples as well. If you are in a couples group, talk about the "one-in-seven" principle and discuss ways you could plan some "holy play" or "holy rest" as a group. Making lifestyle changes sometimes requires the strength that group support provides.

HOW SABBATH REST CAN MAKE
YOUR MARRIAGE BETTER

We know that one large barrier to couples working on their marriages is the lack of time. It's a litany with almost every couple I work with: "We are so busy." "Our lives are so complicated." "Between the demands of our jobs and the demands of our children, we have no time for each other." These statements are all true—Jan and I have said them and felt the reality of them as well. And that's the point! Following the one-in-seven principle gives us quality time together as a couple. It also gives us quality time together as a family. If quality time is the ingredient that provides the context for improving our marriage, then the consistent practice of the Sabbath rest provides the opportunity. It's all part of God's wonderful design!

TO TALK ABOUT TOGETHER

- Discuss together how each of your families observed Sundays while you were growing up. How were your experiences similar or different?
- List the things you do during the week. What are some "don'ts" you could apply to your special one-day-in-seven that would help you make that day different from the rest of the week?

- Because the Sabbath rest we are talking about covers a whole day, talk together about how you will involve your children, both in the planning and in the implementation of what you want to do to make this "one-in-seven" day special for all of you. Talk with them about why attending church is a part of your Sabbath celebration. Discuss also how you will keep the balance between your time as a couple and your time as a family.

SIXTEEN

Finding Strength for the Darkness: *Long-Term Reasons for Spiritual Exercise*

As Gary laid out for me the series of tragedies he had experienced, I began to wonder how I could help him. On the phone he had told me that his wife, Arlene, had recently died of cancer after a long battle with the disease. In the office he told me in detail about their battle. They had tried all the conventional treatments here and had gone to Mexico and tried several alternative treatments there. They had even attended several healing services, which for a short time had seemed to help. But after three years, death ended the battle for her.

When Gary finished telling me about his wife's death, he then went on to tell me that five years earlier his seventeen-year-old son had been killed in a hiking accident and that eighteen years ago, another son had died three months after his birth. He had one other child still living, a twenty-four-year-old daughter.

"You've had a lot of grieving in your life," I said. He nodded in agreement and then after several minutes of silence added, "I think I have grieved a lot. My concern really is that some of my friends think I am in denial about the loss of my sons and my wife. I don't think I am, but I need you to help me see if I am."

As we talked over the next couple of months, it became very clear to me that Gary was not in denial about his losses. He had grieved—deeply and painfully. But there was something else about Gary that seemed rare, and it was perhaps confusing to those who knew him and were concerned about him. There was a depth to his relationship with God that was both unassuming and profound.

When I asked him about how he had developed his relationship with God, he replied, "I think it really started when my first son died as a baby. It was a terrible time for us, but it also drove both Arlene and me to the Lord. We spent hours during the month Todd was in the hospital praying together, fasting, searching the Scriptures—doing anything we could to plead with God for his mercy on our son. After he died, we committed to each other to continue praying together, to spend time fasting, and to meditate on the Scriptures. At first it was part of our effort to understand why Todd had to die. But later it became a part of our relationship with each other and with God. I don't think either of us could have handled Matt's hiking accident without the sense of God's sovereignty that we had nurtured over the years together through our praying and study of the Scriptures."

As I reflected later on Gary's journey, it reminded me of the time some years earlier when I was on the pastoral staff of a church and two of the leaders in the church were critically ill at the same time. I have thought often about the differences between them as they faced death. Prior to their illnesses, both were considered spiritual leaders in the church. But down deep inside they were very different. One died praising God for his goodness right up until he drew his last breath. The other died bitter and angry with God for not healing him.

Gary's experience, along with the markedly different responses of those two church leaders, underlines the fact that, long before we face the periods of darkness in our lives, we need to practice the attitudes of the heart that are deeply connected to Jesus. We need to become spiritually fit through the exercise of spiritual disciplines.

Long before we face darkness in our lives, we need
to practice the attitudes of the heart that
are deeply connected to Jesus.

WHEN THE DARKNESS COMES

Every couple at some time, and probably even several times, will go through periods of darkness. It doesn't have to be as dark as Gary's experiences, but there will be times when it seems that darkness surrounds us and there is no light anywhere. One writer defines this darkness as "a psychological state of great discomfort, precipitated either by external causes like painful loss or trauma, or by inner conflicts leading to depression and a feeling of profound alienation."[1] The darkness of the soul is often accompanied by feelings of worthlessness, fatigue, agitation, and a loss of interest in anything pleasurable.

As the darkness falls all around us, no one is exempt from experiencing some or all of these feelings. When trauma, loss, or inner conflicts descend, they will always knock the wind out of us. We will question, deny, struggle, doubt, and even feel like giving up. It is only human to wonder, especially in the beginning, "Where is God?" But at some point early in the process something happens within those who are in good shape spiritually. Instead of giving in to the feelings of despair and unfairness, our hearts begin to focus on God and his faithfulness. We hold on to

1. Benedict J. Groeschel, *Spiritual Passages* (New York: Crossroad, 1983), 131.

the sovereign God as our caring protector. Just as physical exercise prepares us for strenuous physical activity, so spiritual exercise prepares us for the strenuous spiritual challenges life brings to us.

Paul uses this contrast between physical conditioning and spiritual conditioning in 1 Corinthians 9:25-27.

> *"To win the contest you must deny yourselves many things that would keep you from doing your best. An athlete goes to all this trouble just to win a blue ribbon or a silver cup, but we do it for a heavenly reward that never disappears. So I run straight to the goal with purpose in every step. I fight to win. I'm not just shadow-boxing or playing around. Like an athlete I punish my body, treating it roughly, training it to do what it should, not what it wants to. Otherwise I fear that after enlisting others for the race, I myself might be declared unfit and ordered to stand aside."*

And again, to the Galatians he writes, "And let us not get tired of doing what is right, for after a while we will reap a harvest of blessing if we don't get discouraged and give up" (6:9). He tells Timothy to "follow the Lord's rules for doing his work, just as an athlete either follows the rules or is disqualified and wins no prize" (2 Tim. 2:5).

What happens in the midst of the darkness when we have exercised our spiritual "muscles"? Our memory is centered on God in spite of the darkness. With the psalmist our voice, deep within us, begins to say, "But as for me, I will sing each morning about your power and mercy. For you have been my high tower of refuge, a place of safety in the day of my distress. O my Strength, to you I sing my praises; for you are my high tower of safety, my God of mercy" (Ps. 59:16-17). We take hold of God's faithfulness and begin to hope and trust in him. Our faith becomes stronger, and its roots go deeper. As the darkness strips away our self-sufficiency, all the other voices within are silenced except for the voice of God.

Our memory is centered on God
in spite of the darkness.

We are not exempt from these periods of darkness, even when we, as a couple, are conditioned spiritually. But what we find on the other side of the darkness will be a greater knowledge of God, as well as of ourselves. We will also find a deepening sense of spiritual intimacy with each other. When we go through the darkness unprepared, what we find on the other side will be continuing pain, bitterness, anger, disappointment, and a growing cynicism about our faith.

We can describe these two approaches to the darkness like this:

THE DARKNESS OF THE SOUL

	Unprepared	Prepared
STAGE 1:	Despair Discomfort Depression	Despair Discomfort Depression
STAGE 2:	Question God Doubts and fears	Question God Doubts and fears
STAGE 3:	Give up on God Give up on faith	Memory centered on God Take hold of God
STAGE 4:	We get through based on self-sufficiency	We get through based on God's sufficiency
STAGE 5:	Left with bitterness, anger, disappointment, and cynicism	Greater knowledge of God Greater knowledge of self Deepening spiritual intimacy

Think of the darkness of the soul as the running of a race. At the beginning, everyone is able to run. One can hardly tell the difference between those who have prepared and trained for the race and those who haven't. But as the race continues, those who haven't prepared will begin to struggle, pushing themselves, drawing merely on what they have within *themselves,* only to drop out of the race and give up in bitterness and disappointment.

On the other hand, those who have prepared and have trained will hit that same point where they struggle and feel like quitting. But because of their conditioning, they will find their "second wind" and be able to continue on, drawing from a strength that seems to be beyond themselves. Only they will know the joy of finishing the race.

What Really Makes a Marriage Christian

We started in the beginning of this book with the question, "What is it that makes a marriage Christian?" Our answer was that as a couple, we are seeking to restore to our marriage what was lost back in the Garden of Eden—the spiritual intimacy Adam and Eve shared together with God. Now, many pages later, I hope we have not only shown the importance of our answer to that question, but have also given you some important and practical insights into how you can develop and enjoy that spiritual intimacy within your marriage.

As I prepared to write this chapter, Jan and I were talking about the benefits we've experienced using the spiritual disciplines in our marriage. I said to her, "I wish somehow that couples could understand the value of using the spiritual disciplines to develop spiritual intimacy early in their marriage. It could really make a difference." Let me describe three of these benefits for you.

An Awareness of the Sacredness of Marriage

It's so easy to forget that God is to be at the heart of our marriage, especially in our culture of "me-ism." We need to be reminded on a regular basis that, in the words of the wedding ceremony, "Marriage is a holy estate, ordained by God and blessed by our Lord Jesus Christ." When we apply spiritual practice to our marriage, it grows in these sacred dimensions. Not only do we care for the relationship more conscientiously, but we also receive from the relationship a deeper satisfaction that is rooted in eternal purposes.

When we apply spiritual practice to our marriage, we receive from the relationship a deeper satisfaction that is rooted in eternal purposes.

A Strengthening of the Bond between the Married Partners

We were profoundly aware of this during and following our silent retreat. The spiritual and emotional bond we felt at that time has stayed with us. We believe the reason it has is that through the work of God's Holy Spirit, that bondedness went deep within each of us and within our souls. When our mind, our heart, *and* our soul are involved, we tap into roots that go deep and give us added strength.

A Continual Drawing into the Very Presence of God

We don't practice our spirituality in order to somehow gain God's favor; we practice because, in God's grace, he has already bestowed upon us his favor, and he wants to involve us in his work so that *we* can be blessed. What greater privilege can a couple have than to share with God in his activities and work?

Jan's and my story has some similarities to Gary's experiences. Our darkness wasn't related to the death of a loved one but to the

PERIENCING GOD TOGETHER

struggles of one of our children. For several years we struggled with each other, and then somehow we gradually pulled back from opposing each other and started to work on our shared spirituality as a basis for dealing with our "dark night of the soul" of that time. Gradually we were able to internalize and personalize the words of the psalmist:

> O God, listen to me! Hear my prayer! For wherever I am, though far away at the ends of the earth, I will cry to you for help. When my heart is faint and overwhelmed, lead me to the mighty, towering Rock of safety. For you are my refuge, a high tower where my enemies can never reach me. Ps. 61:1-3

We read a similar statement of faith in the midst of the darkness in the next psalm:

> I stand silently before the Lord, waiting for him to rescue me. For salvation comes from him alone. Yes, he alone is my Rock, my rescuer, defense and fortress. Why then should I be tense with fear when troubles come? Ps. 62:1-2

These are great promises that we tried to hold onto many times during our period of trouble and darkness. But we found in our experience that the reality of promises like these only became rooted in our hearts and memories when we had started the process of disciplining our spiritual muscles through the exercise of the spiritual disciplines. They did not represent dry, dull routines. Rather, they became times of great joy, especially when we found ourselves engulfed in the darkness.

The benefits are well worth the effort! We encourage you to participate with God and give the Holy Spirit the opportunity to transform your marriage into a deep, spiritual partnership. As you step off the curb and into the grand parade together, keep these important truths in mind:

1. We must recognize that God is already at work all around us.
2. Because of the high priority that God places on marriage, he cares deeply about us and our marriage, and he invites us *as a married couple* to join him in his work—already in progress.
3. There are a variety of ways—called spiritual disciplines— we can participate with God, and each of them can deepen our personal faith, as well as deepen our sense of intimacy with each other and together with God.
4. These spiritual disciplines will require at least two things from us. First, that we face our own fears and defenses, especially those we encounter in our marriage relationship; and second, that we adjust our priorities and activities.
5. The deepening experience of our spiritual intimacy with God together will prepare us for a life of obedience, especially when we encounter the "dark nights of the soul."

TO TALK ABOUT TOGETHER

- Describe what to you has been a period of soul darkness—for you individually, or for your marriage partnership. What helped you emotionally? What strengthened your relationship with one another? What gave you spiritual refreshment?
- In what ways have periods of darkness strengthened you spiritually?
- Discuss the three benefits (described in this chapter) that we can experience through the spiritual disciplines. What benefits are you beginning to experience as a result of working through this book?